# Table of Contents

# COPYRIGHT

# Introduction

Congratulations on wanting to learn more about the stock market! If you are looking for clear, relevant and useful information to help you enlarge your financial business vocabulary, you have come to the right place. As the saying goes, words have power and money talks.

Note that this book is not about financial advice. It is written in plain English for intermediate and advanced ESL Business English students who want to have fun while gaining a deeper understanding of financial vocabulary and how the stock market works. While the primary emphasis is on North America, the book also provides a brief overview of global markets.

Business English can be formal and serious, but why not make learning fun? This book is a hands-on approach that emphasizes practical application. By playing with words and actively using financial vocabulary, you'll gain a deeper understanding of the stock market and improve your ability to discuss it confidently. This interactive method will also maximize your vocabulary retention. In other words, by actively using the new vocabulary, you'll remember more of it, and better and longer.

This book is designed to optimize your vocabulary learning by incorporating principles from neurolinguistics, including spaced repetition. Repeatedly exposing you to keywords and expressions at strategic intervals, creates the ideal conditions for acquiring new vocabulary and solidifying your understanding. By mastering the terminology used in the stock market and expanding your business vocabulary, you'll feel more confident and better informed during financial discussions.

# Introduction

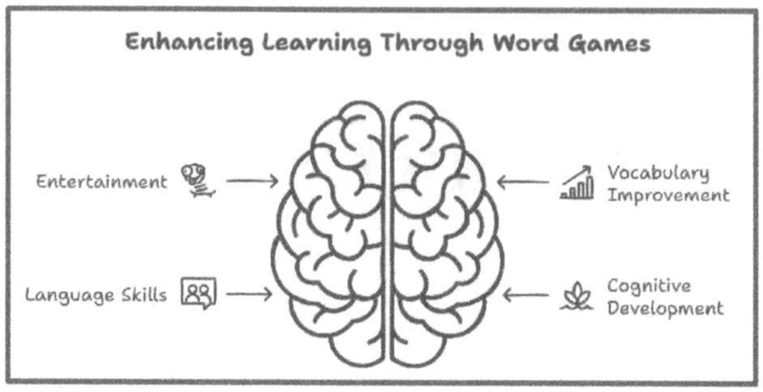


This book is organized into eight chapters, covering a comprehensive range of topics related to the stock market. The chapters are presented in a logical sequence:

1. **The 11 Sectors of the Economy:** Introduces the different sectors of the economy and their impact on the stock market.
2. **Who Participates in the Stock Market?** Explores the various types of participants in the stock market, including individuals, institutions, and corporations.
3. **Trading Instruments (securities and equities):** Defines and explains different types of securities and equities traded in the stock market.
4. **The Different Types of Trading:** Discusses various trading strategies and approaches, such as buying and holding, day trading, and swing trading.
5. **Bull and Bear Markets:** Covers the concepts of bull and bear markets and their implications for investors.
6. **Fundamental Analysis:** Explains the process of analyzing a company's financial health and prospects to make investment decisions.
7. **Technical Analysis:** Introduces the use of charts and patterns to identify potential trading opportunities.
8. **Stock Market Idioms:** Provides a list of common stock market idioms and their meanings.

Each chapter uses ten types of engaging and interactive word games and exercises to help you learn stock market vocabulary effectively.

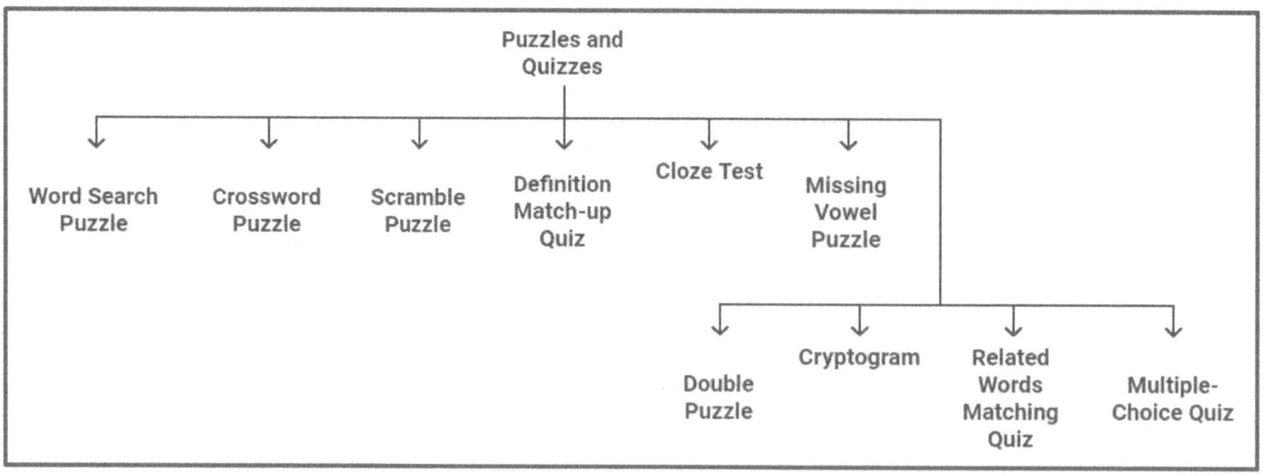

# How Can this Book Help You?

What are some other ways in which this book can help you? Understanding the stock market can be important for Business English students for several reasons:

1. The stock market is a key component of the global economy, and understanding how it works can give students a **better understanding of how businesses operate and how economic conditions can affect them**.

2. Many business professionals need to have a basic understanding of the stock market in order to **make informed decisions about their own investments or the investments of their company**.

3. The stock market is often used as a metaphor in business discussions, so having a basic understanding of how it works can help students **better understand and participate in business conversations**.

4. Understanding the stock market can also be useful for students who are interested in **pursuing careers in finance or business**, as it is a fundamental concept in these fields.

## Did You Know?

Did you know that it may take as many as 10 to 20 exposures for a new word or expression to be fully committed to long-term memory? This can vary based on factors such as age, familiarity with related concepts, level of interest, and context of encounter. To best commit new information to memory, repetition is important because it helps to establish a strong foundation of knowledge that you can build upon. As you continue to encounter and repeat the new information over time, it becomes more and more ingrained in your long-term memory.

# On a More Personal Level

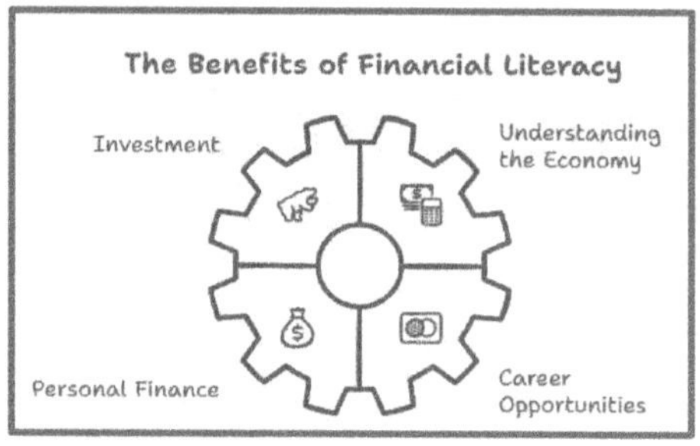


On a more personal level, we can add:

1. **Investment**: The stock market can be a way to potentially earn money through investing in publicly traded companies. By learning about the stock market and how it works, you can make more informed decisions about which companies to invest in and potentially earn a return on your investment.
2. **Understanding the economy**: The stock market is often used as a barometer for the overall health of the economy. By learning about the stock market, you can gain a better understanding of the current economic climate and how it may impact your personal financial situation.
3. **Personal finance**: Understanding the stock market can also help you make better decisions about your own personal finance and retirement planning. For example, you may decide to invest in a 401(k), RRSP or other retirement accounts, which can be invested in a variety of stock and bond funds.
4. **Career opportunities**: There are many careers that involve working with the stock market, such as stockbroker, financial analyst, and portfolio manager. Learning about the stock market can help you understand these careers and potentially pursue them as a career path.

Overall, learning about the stock market can help you improve your financial literacy in English and make more informed decisions about your future. Whether you're considering investments, saving for retirement, or exploring a career in finance, understanding the stock market provides valuable insights and tools to navigate the complexities of the financial world and show a solid grasp of financial matters.

Are you ready to start learning? Let's get started!

# What is the Stock Market?

Simply put, the stock market is a place where people can buy and sell stocks, which are small pieces of ownership in a company. When you buy a stock, you own a tiny part of that company, and you can make money if the company does well. The stock market also helps companies raise money by selling stocks to people. The stock market is important because it helps companies get the money they need to grow and run their business, and it gives people a chance to earn money by investing in stocks. There are many different stock markets around the world, such as the NYSE (New York Stock Exchange) and NASDAQ (National Association of Securities Dealers Automated Quotations) in the U.S.

**Let's Start with an Easy Quiz!**

**1) What is the stock market?**
a) A place where people can buy and sell cars
b) A place where people can buy and sell houses
c) A place where people can buy and sell stocks
d) A place where people can buy and sell sports stuff

**2) When you buy a stock, what do you own a little of?**
a) A company
b) A house
c) A car
d) A sports team

**3) How can you make money by investing in stocks?**
a) If the sports team does well
b) If the value of the house goes up
c) If the value of the car goes up
d) If the company's stocks go up in value

**4) Why is the stock market important?**
a) It helps people buy and sell houses at a good price.
b) It helps companies raise money by selling stocks, and it gives people a chance to make money by investing in stocks.
c) It helps people buy and sell cars at a good price.
d) It helps people buy and sell luxury stuff at a good price.

**5) Name two stock markets in the U.S.**
a) London Stock Exchange and Tokyo Stock Exchange
b) S&P 500 and Dow Jones Industrial Average
c) NYSE (New York Stock Exchange) and NASDAQ (National Association of Securities Dealers Automated Quotations)
d) Shanghai Stock Exchange and Hong Kong Stock Exchange

*See Solution on p. 172*

# What is the Stock Market?

## North America

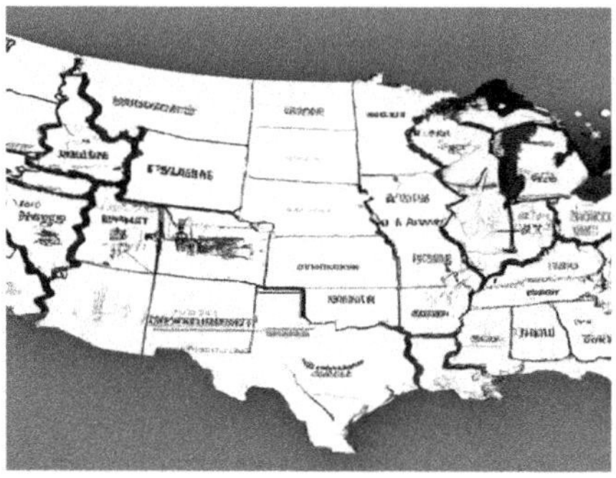

**The United States:** The NYSE (New York Stock Exchange) and NASDAQ (National Association of Securities Dealers Automated Quotations) are both stock markets located in the United States. The NYSE is the largest stock exchange in the world by market capitalization, and it is home to many well-known companies. The NASDAQ, on the other hand, is known for having a high number of technology-based companies listed on it. Both stock markets allow people to buy and sell stocks in publicly traded companies.

**Canada:** The Toronto Stock Exchange (TSX) is the largest stock exchange in Canada. It is located in Toronto, Ontario and is home to many Canadian-based companies, as well as some international firms. The TSX is known for its diverse range of industries, including mining, oil and gas, financial services, and technology. It is also home to the TSX Venture Exchange, which is a platform for emerging and small-cap companies. The TSX is a member of the World Federation of Exchanges and is an important financial hub in Canada and the broader North American market.

**Mexico**: The Mexican Stock Exchange (Bolsa Mexicana de Valores, or BMV) is the largest and most important stock exchange in Mexico. It is located in Mexico City and is home to many Mexican-based companies, as well as some international firms. The BMV is known for its diverse range of industries, including banking, energy, telecommunications, and consumer goods. It is an important financial hub in Mexico and is a member of the World Federation of Exchanges. The BMV is also linked to other stock exchanges in the region, such as NYSE and the Santiago Stock Exchange in Chile, through the Latin American Integrated Market (MILA).

# What is the Stock Market?

## The World

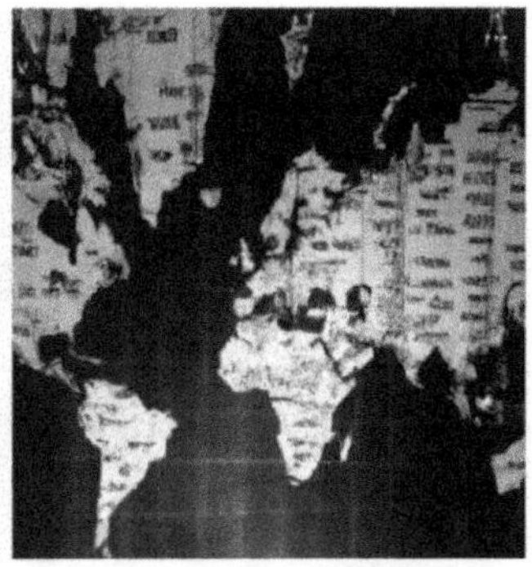

**Global market:** There are many stock markets around the world that are considered to be important in terms of the size and liquidity of their markets, and the number and size of the companies listed on them. Some of the most important stock markets after the NYSE and NASDAQ include:

1. **The Tokyo Stock Exchange (TSE) in Japan:** The largest stock exchange in Asia which is home to many Japanese-based companies, as well as some international firms.

2. **The London Stock Exchange (LSE) in the United Kingdom:** The largest stock exchange in Europe which is known for its diverse range of industries, including finance, energy, and mining.

3. **The Shanghai Stock Exchange (SSE) in China:** The largest stock exchange in China which is home to many Chinese-based companies, as well as some international firms.

4. **The Hong Kong Stock Exchange (HKEX) in China:** The second-largest stock exchange in China which is known for its strong focus on financial and real estate companies.

5. **The Bombay Stock Exchange (BSE) in India:** The oldest stock exchange in India which is home to many Indian-based companies, as well as some international firms.

6. **The Euronext Stock Exchange in Europe:** A pan-European stock exchange that is made up of several different exchanges, including the Amsterdam Stock Exchange, the Brussels Stock Exchange, and the Paris Stock Exchange.

7. **The Sydney Stock Exchange (SSX) in Australia:** The largest stock exchange in Australia known for its strong focus on mining and energy companies.

# What is the Stock Market?

## The World

There are many other stock exchanges around the world that are considered to be important in their respective regions. Some examples include:

8. **The São Paulo Stock Exchange (B3) in Brazil:** The largest stock exchange in South America which is home to many Brazilian-based companies, as well as some international firms.

9. **The Santiago Stock Exchange (Bolsa de Comercio de Santiago) in Chile:** The largest stock exchange in Chile which is home to many Chilean-based companies, as well as some international firms.

10. **The Johannesburg Stock Exchange (JSE) in South Africa:** The largest stock exchange in Africa which is known for its strong focus on mining and energy companies.

11. **The National Stock Exchange of India (NSE) in India:** The second-largest stock exchange in India which is known for its diverse range of industries, including finance, technology, and consumer goods.

12. **The Korean Stock Exchange (KSE) in South Korea:** The largest stock exchange in South Korea which is home to many Korean-based companies, as well as some international firms.

13. **The Taiwan Stock Exchange (TWSE) in Taiwan:** The largest stock exchange in Taiwan which is known for its strong focus on technology and electronics companies.

14. **The Australian Securities Exchange (ASX) in Australia:** The second-largest stock exchange in Australia which is known for its diverse range of industries, including mining, energy, and financial services.

There are many other stock exchanges around the world that are also important in their respective regions, and the importance of a particular exchange may vary depending on the specific industry or sector being considered.

# The 11 Sectors of the Economy

**There are 11 sectors of the economy:**

- Healthcare
- Materials
- Real Estate
- Consumer Staples
- Consumer Discretionary
- Utilities
- Energy
- Industrials
- Consumer Services
- Financials
- Technology

### Did You Know?

The 11 sectors of the economy are classified as **primary**, **secondary**, and **tertiary**? The primary sector includes industries that extract raw materials from the earth, such as agriculture, forestry, and mining. The secondary sector includes industries that transform raw materials into finished products, such as manufacturing and construction. The tertiary sector includes industries that provide services, such as healthcare, education, and transportation.

**What is the relationship between the stock market and the 11 sectors of the economy?**

The stock market is a place where people buy and sell shares of companies. These companies can be in different industries, such as energy, healthcare, or technology. The stock market can show how well the economy is doing overall. When the stock market is doing well, it means that companies are doing well and the economy is strong. When the stock market is not doing well, it means that companies are struggling and the economy is not as strong. Companies can also use the stock market to raise money for their business by selling shares of their company to investors.

## Word Search Puzzle #1 - The 11 Sectors of the Economy

**Find the 11 sectors of the economy words in the list below**

| C | W | K | M | Z | W | I | I | E | J | O | Z | S | A | S | X |
|---|---|---|---|---|---|---|---|---|---|---|---|---|---|---|---|
| O | M | D | A | D | T | Z | N | E | F | T | G | K | F | L | S |
| N | I | I | T | H | E | L | D | Q | B | H | A | O | H | E | R |
| S | Q | S | E | E | C | I | K | O | Y | G | C | V | L | O | E |
| U | I | C | R | A | H | U | L | I | V | C | C | P | U | V | A |
| M | N | R | I | L | N | C | A | K | Z | Y | A | S | T | T | L |
| E | D | E | A | T | O | O | D | S | B | T | X | T | I | T | E |
| R | U | T | L | H | L | N | W | M | S | D | P | V | L | U | S |
| S | S | I | S | C | O | S | S | R | S | R | U | G | I | H | T |
| E | T | O | N | A | G | U | E | K | G | H | Y | K | T | V | A |
| R | R | N | R | R | Y | M | L | M | M | G | G | M | I | G | T |
| V | I | A | J | E | U | E | E | Z | R | Q | U | K | E | F | E |
| I | A | R | T | S | E | R | A | E | R | N | F | C | S | C | J |
| C | L | Y | N | L | F | I | N | A | N | C | I | A | L | S | W |
| E | S | O | L | O | C | E | W | Z | D | U | E | N | Q | Y | X |
| S | C | G | U | A | A | N | Q | Y | G | H | O | Y | X | R | Q |

CONSUMER
CONSUMER SERVICES
CONSUMER STAPLES
DISCRETIONARY
ENERGY
FINANCIALS
HEALTHCARE
INDUSTRIALS
MATERIALS
REAL ESTATE
TECHNOLOGY
UTILITIES

*See Solution on p. 172*

# Crossword #1 - The 11 Sectors of the Economy

**Fill in the answers to the clues provided, using the intersecting words and letter counts as hints.**

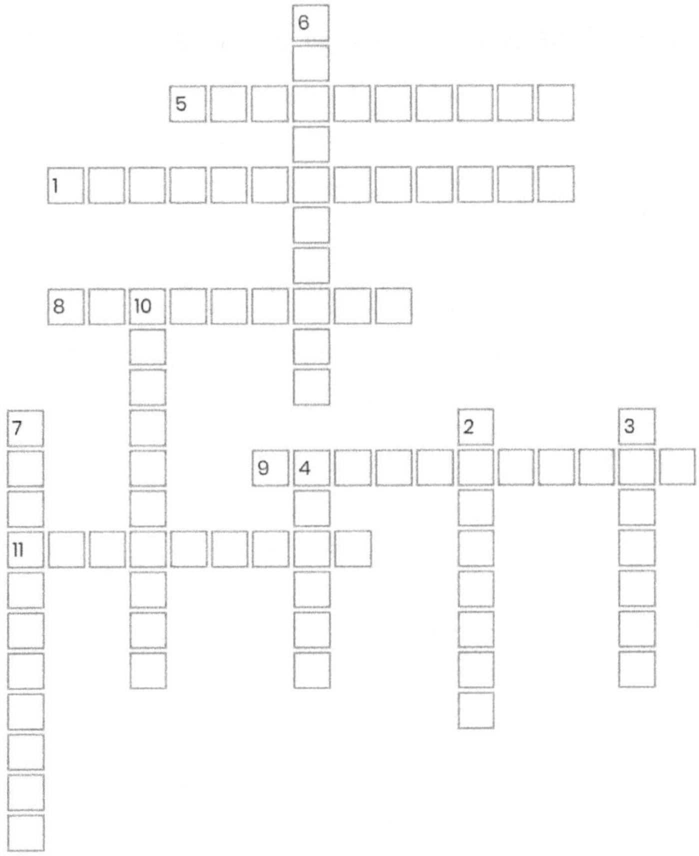

Across

**[1]** Consumer ________ is about luxury goods and recreation.

**[5]** About money-related services such as banks and insurance.

**[8]** About raw materials such as chemicals and metals.

**[9]** About property ownership and management.

**[11]** About services such as water and electricity.

Down

**[2]** Consumer ___________ is about services such as education and healthcare.

**[3]** Consumer ____________ is about essential goods and services such as food and household products.

**[4]** About energy production and distribution.

**[6]** About health-related products and services.

**[7]** About manufacturing, construction, and transportation-related goods and services.

**[10]** About IT products and services.

*See Solution on p. 172*

## Scramble Puzzle #1 - The 11 Sectors of the Economy

### Unscramble the 11 sectors of the economy words in the list below

CESMNOUR DRTESRNIAOICY

CSEUNOMR SLTAEPS

TCOELOGNHY

HAEHCRALTE

MTRALAIES

IASRUDLNTIS

ERGENY

UEIITTLIS

ALER EASTTE

CEOUMNSR SRIECEVS

**Did You Know?**

Did you know that the service sector is the largest contributor to the global economy? This sector includes industries like finance, insurance, and real estate, healthcare, education, and transportation.

*See Solution on p. 172*

# Definition Match-Up #1

The 11 Sectors of the Economy 1

**Associate the Sectors of the Economy to their Definitions:**

| | | | |
|---|---|---|---|
| **1** | Healthcare | **A** | Goods and services for consumer consumption, such as apparel, media, and retail. |
| **2** | Materials | **B** | Services to consumers, such as retail stores, restaurants, and hotels. |
| **3** | Real Estate | **C** | Goods and services that are essential for everyday life, such as food, household goods, and personal care products. |
| **4** | Consumer Staples | **D** | Energy, such as oil, gas, and renewable energy. |
| **5** | Consumer Discretionary | **E** | Financial services, such as banks, insurance, and real estate. |
| **6** | Utilities | **F** | Goods and services related to healthcare, such as pharmaceuticals, medical devices, and hospitals. |
| **7** | Energy | **G** | Goods, such as aerospace, construction, and transportation. |
| **8** | Industrials | **H** | Raw materials, such as metals, chemicals, and forestry products. |
| **9** | Consumer Services | **I** | Realty industry, such as property development, management, and ownership. |
| **10** | Financials | **J** | Innovation products and services, including software, hardware, and telecommunications. |
| **11** | Technology | **K** | Essential services such as electricity, gas, and water. |

*See Solution on p. 173*

# Cloze Test #1

## Fill In the Blanks Using the 11 Sectors of the Economy

| Financials - Consumer Discretionary - Consumer Staples - Energy - Healthcare - Industrials - Materials - Real Estate - Technology - Consumer Services - Utilities |
|---|

1. ________ is a vital industry that provides essential clinical services to people around the world.
2. ________ are the raw ingredients that are used to create a wide variety of products, from buildings to consumer goods.
3. ________ involves the buying, selling, and management of properties such as homes, offices, and retail spaces.
4. ________ are everyday items that people need to live, such as food, clothing, and personal care products.
5. ________ refers to products and services that people can choose to buy, such as electronics, vacations, and luxury goods.
6. ________ provide essential services like electricity, gas, and water to households and businesses.
7. ________ refers to the production, distribution, and use of power, including fossil fuels and renewable sources.
8. ________ include a wide range of businesses, from manufacturing to transportation.
9. ________ include industries such as retail, tourism, and entertainment.
10. ________ encompass banks, insurance companies, and investment firms.
11. ________ encompasses the development and use of computer systems, software, and networks.

*See Solution on p. 173*

# Missing Vowel #1

## Learn about the 11 Sectors of the Stock Market

| Puzzle | Clue |
| --- | --- |
| C _ N S _ M _ R   S _ R V _ C _ S | About services such as education and healthcare. |
| _ T _ L _ T _ _ S | About services such as water and electricity. |
| C _ N S _ M _ R   D _ S C R _ T _ _ N _ R Y | About luxury goods and recreation. |
| F _ N _ N C _ _ L S | About money-related services such as banks and insurance. |
| H _ _ L T H C _ R _ | About health-related products and services. |
| T _ C H N _ L _ G Y | About IT products and services. |
| _ N _ R G Y | About energy production and distribution. |
| M _ T _ R _ _ L S | About raw materials such as chemicals and metals. |
| R _ _ L   _ S T _ T _ | About property ownership and management. |
| _ N D _ S T R _ _ L S | About manufacturing, construction, and transportation-related goods and services. |

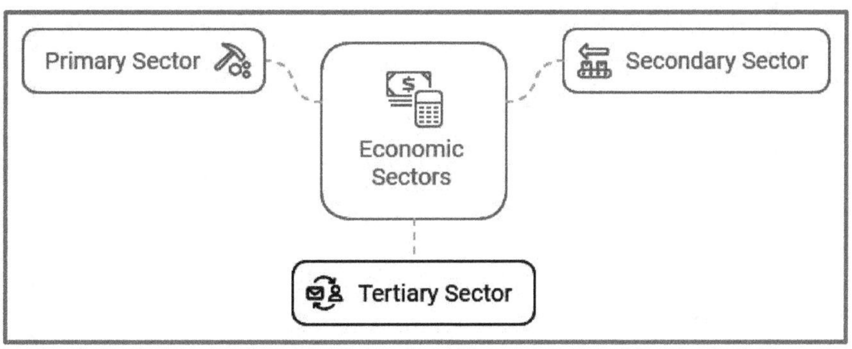


See Solution on p. 173

# Double Puzzle #1

## A list of words that describe the 11 sectors of the economy

HLACHEARTE (box 1 numbered 2)

MRLTAEIAS (box 1 numbered 11)

ELRA EATTSE (box 3 numbered 12)

CEUNOSMR SLEAPTS (boxes numbered 5, 3)

CSMEOUNR DNEIIASCRTROY (boxes numbered 16, 13)

UTIILETIS (boxes numbered 1, 6, 15)

EEGNRY

ILTRUSANIDS

CUSMNEOR SECIREVS (box numbered 8)

FCINAINLAS

TNHOLCOGEY (box numbered 7)

_ _ _   _ _ _ _ K   _ _ _ K _ _

1 2 3   5 6 7 8 9   11 12 13 14 15 16

## Did You Know?

This book uses spaced repetition, a learning technique in which previously learned words and expressions are reviewed at increasing intervals of time. The idea is that by spacing out your review sessions, you will be able to commit information to long-term memory more effectively.

*See Solution on p. 173*

## Cryptogram #1 - A PIECE OF ADVICE FROM WARREN BUFFET

| A | B | C | D | E | F | G | H | I | J | K | L | M | N | O | P | Q | R | S | T | U | V | W | X | Y | Z |
|---|---|---|---|---|---|---|---|---|---|---|---|---|---|---|---|---|---|---|---|---|---|---|---|---|---|
| | | | | | | | | | | | | | | | | | | | | | | | | | |

Y    R Y D D    L S D D    G W T    Z W R    L W

J S P W H S    U Y P Z    P D W C S    L Z S

N W W U C    J S    E S B U E T D    R Z S Q

W L Z S U C    B U S    I U S S N G    J S

I U S S N G    R Z S Q    W L Z S U C    B U S

E S B U E T D

- Warren Buffett

*See Solution on p. 174*

# Related Words Matching #1

### Associate the Sectors of the Economy to their Family of Words:

| | | | |
|---|---|---|---|
| 1 | Consumer Discretionary | A | software, hardware, computers, electronics, internet |
| 2 | Consumer Services | B | electricity, gas, water, sanitation, telecommunications |
| 3 | Consumer Staples | C | raw materials, metals, minerals, chemicals, plastics |
| 4 | Energy | D | retail, hospitality, restaurants, travel, entertainment |
| 5 | Financials | E | medicine, treatment, hospitals, clinics, pharmaceuticals |
| 6 | Healthcare | F | oil, gas, renewable energy, fossil fuels, electricity |
| 7 | Industrials | G | food, beverages, household goods, groceries, toiletries |
| 8 | Materials | H | property, housing, land, commercial, residential |
| 9 | Real Estate | I | luxury goods, leisure, entertainment, fashion, retail |
| 10 | Technology | J | banking, insurance, investment, finance, stocks |
| 11 | Utilities | K | manufacturing, construction, machinery, transportation, engineering |

*See Solution on p. 174*

**The Importance of the 11 Sectors of the Economy**

Understanding the 11 sectors of the economy is important for business students, particularly those who are learning English as a second language, because it provides a framework for understanding how different industries and businesses operate and how they fit into the larger economic system. This knowledge can help students make informed decisions about their career paths, understand the economic forces that shape the business world, and develop strategies for success in the global economy. Additionally, understanding the different sectors of the economy can help students better understand the news and current events related to business and finance, and make informed decisions about investments and other financial matters. Overall, understanding the 11 sectors of the economy is an essential part of a well-rounded education in business and economics.

# Multiple-Choice Quiz #1: Circle the Correct Answer

1. **What is the main reason why it is important for business students to understand the 11 sectors of the economy?**
a) To make informed decisions about career paths
b) To develop strategies for success in the global economy
c) To understand how different industries and businesses operate
d) All of the above

2. **How can understanding the 11 sectors of the economy help students better understand current events related to business and finance?**
a) By providing a framework for understanding how different industries and businesses operate
b) By helping students make informed decisions about investments and other financial matters
c) By helping students understand the economic forces that shape the business world
d) All of the above

3. **What type of education in business and economics is considered well-rounded?**
a) An education that includes an understanding of the 11 sectors of the economy
b) An education that focuses solely on financial matters
c) An education that focuses solely on marketing and sales
d) An education that focuses solely on management and leadership

4. **Which of the following is NOT a way that understanding the 11 sectors of the economy can benefit business students?**
a) It can help them make informed decisions about career paths
b) It can help them develop strategies for success in the global economy
c) It can help them better understand the news and current events related to business and finance
d) It can help them understand the technical aspects of running a business

**The Importance of the 11 Sectors of the Economy**

Understanding the 11 sectors of the economy is important for business students, particularly those who are learning English as a second language, because it provides a framework for understanding how different industries and businesses operate and how they fit into the larger economic system. This knowledge can help students make informed decisions about their career paths, understand the economic forces that shape the business world, and develop strategies for success in the global economy. Additionally, understanding the different sectors of the economy can help students better understand the news and current events related to business and finance, and make informed decisions about investments and other financial matters. Overall, understanding the 11 sectors of the economy is an essential part of a well-rounded education in business and economics.

# Multiple-Choice Quiz #1: Circle the Correct Answer

5. **What is NOT a sector of the economy?**
a) Agriculture
b) Manufacturing
c) Healthcare
d) Social media

6. **Which sector of the economy includes businesses that extract and process raw materials, such as coal, oil, and minerals?**
a) Agriculture
b) Manufacturing
c) Energy
d) Construction

7. **Which sector of the economy includes businesses that provide transportation services, such as airlines, trucking companies, and public transportation?**
a) Transportation
b) Retail
c) Healthcare
d) Finance

8. **Which sector of the economy includes businesses that provide financial services, such as banks, investment firms, and insurance companies?**
a) Retail
b) Finance
c) Healthcare
d) Construction

9. **Which sector of the economy includes businesses that provide healthcare services, such as hospitals, clinics, and nursing homes?**
a) Finance
b) Healthcare
c) Manufacturing
d) Agriculture

10. **Which sector of the economy includes businesses that provide recreational and tourism services, such as hotels, restaurants, and theme parks?**
a) Retail
b) Finance
c) Healthcare
d) Leisure and Hospitality

*See Solution on p. 174*

# The 7 Participants in the Stock Market

**There are 7 Participants in the stock market:**

- Companies
- Investors
- Brokerages
- Exchanges
- Regulators
- Market makers
- Analysts

**Companies**: A company is a legal entity that is formed to engage in business activities. Companies can be publicly traded, meaning that they have issued stock that is traded on a stock exchange, or they can be privately held. Publicly traded companies are required to disclose certain financial and other information to the public, such as their earnings and financial statements.

**Investors**: Investors are individuals or organizations that buy securities, such as stocks or bonds, with the expectation of earning a return on their investment. Investors may be motivated by various factors, such as the desire to earn income or to achieve capital appreciation.

**Brokerages**: A brokerage is a financial services firm that helps clients buy and sell securities. Brokerages may be full-service firms that offer a wide range of financial products and services, or they may be discount brokerages that offer more limited services at a lower cost.

# The 7 Participants in the Stock Market

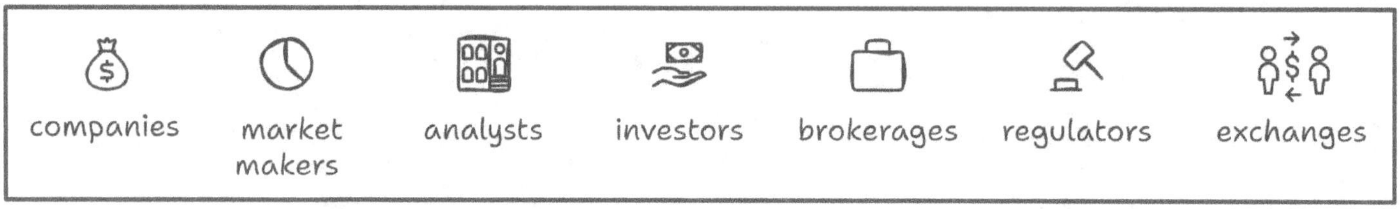


**Exchanges**: An exchange is a marketplace where securities, such as stocks, bonds, and derivatives, are bought and sold. Some of the largest exchanges in the world include the New York Stock Exchange (NYSE), the NASDAQ, and the Tokyo Stock Exchange (TSE).

**Regulators**: Regulators are government agencies or other organizations that are responsible for overseeing and regulating the financial markets. Some examples of financial market regulators include the Securities and Exchange Commission (SEC) in the United States and the Financial Conduct Authority (FCA) in the United Kingdom.

**Market makers**: A market maker is a financial institution or individual that stands ready to buy or sell securities at any time, acting as a "middleman" between buyers and sellers. Market makers help to provide liquidity to the markets by ensuring that there are always willing buyers and sellers for a particular security.

**Analysts**: Analysts are professionals who study and evaluate financial and economic data in order to make recommendations to investors about which securities to buy or sell. Analysts may work for brokerage firms, investment banks, or other financial institutions, and they may specialize in a particular industry or sector.

## Word Search Puzzle #2 - The 7 Participants in the Stock Market

**Find the 7 participants of the stock market in the list below:**

| | | | | | | | | | | | | | | | |
|---|---|---|---|---|---|---|---|---|---|---|---|---|---|---|---|
| O | V | R | K | W | Q | F | B | M | M | H | Q | G | H | P | Y |
| W | S | E | G | A | R | E | K | O | R | B | V | Q | L | Z | A |
| K | T | L | F | C | O | M | P | A | N | I | E | S | H | K | Q |
| E | O | S | N | M | L | W | B | X | Y | A | K | E | W | X | T |
| B | P | R | M | A | H | F | H | C | F | Z | P | T | N | E | M |
| C | F | E | A | M | S | R | O | T | S | E | V | N | I | L | T |
| E | A | K | B | I | K | I | Q | Z | D | X | F | E | Y | S | N |
| X | O | A | T | Z | S | Y | S | W | Y | C | U | Z | X | R | H |
| C | C | M | L | G | Z | T | F | O | U | F | R | N | R | O | F |
| H | I | T | O | P | A | P | L | P | J | Y | N | M | H | T | G |
| A | G | E | O | W | A | N | A | L | Y | S | T | S | C | A | M |
| N | U | K | D | K | U | Q | J | Q | D | K | A | S | L | L | S |
| G | Z | R | L | A | A | J | J | H | C | P | D | H | E | U | S |
| E | D | A | F | Y | M | U | U | T | K | Y | U | B | O | G | G |
| S | Y | M | M | B | K | K | C | N | X | V | P | N | C | E | I |
| I | V | J | Q | Z | L | Y | B | L | D | U | N | S | Q | R | G |

ANALYSTS
COMPANIES
INVESTORS
REGULATORS
BROKERAGES
EXCHANGES
MARKET MAKERS

*See Solution on p. 174*

# Crossword Puzzle #2

## Learn about the 7 Participants in the Stock Market

Across

**[2]** Individuals or organizations that buy securities, such as stocks or bonds, with the expectation of earning a return on their investment.

**[4]** A marketplace where securities, such as stocks, bonds, and derivatives, are bought and sold.

**[6]** A financial institution or individual that stands ready to buy or sell securities at any time, acting as a "middleman" between buyers and sellers.

**[7]** Professionals who study and evaluate financial and economic data in order to make recommendations to investors about which securities to buy or sell.

Down

**[1]** A legal entity that is formed to engage in business activities.

**[3]** A financial services firm that helps clients buy and sell securities.

**[5]** Government agencies or other organizations that are responsible for overseeing the financial markets.

*See Solution on p. 175*

## Scramble #2 - The 7 Participants in the Stock Market

**Uncramble the words in the list below:**

CPIMOENAS □□□□□□□□□

IESVORTNS □□□□□□□□□

BOAGRKEERS □□□□□□□□□□

EEXANCHGS □□□□□□□□□

ROALTEGRUS □□□□□□□□□□

MKERAT MRAKES □□□□□□ □□□□□□

ATLYNASS □□□□□□□□

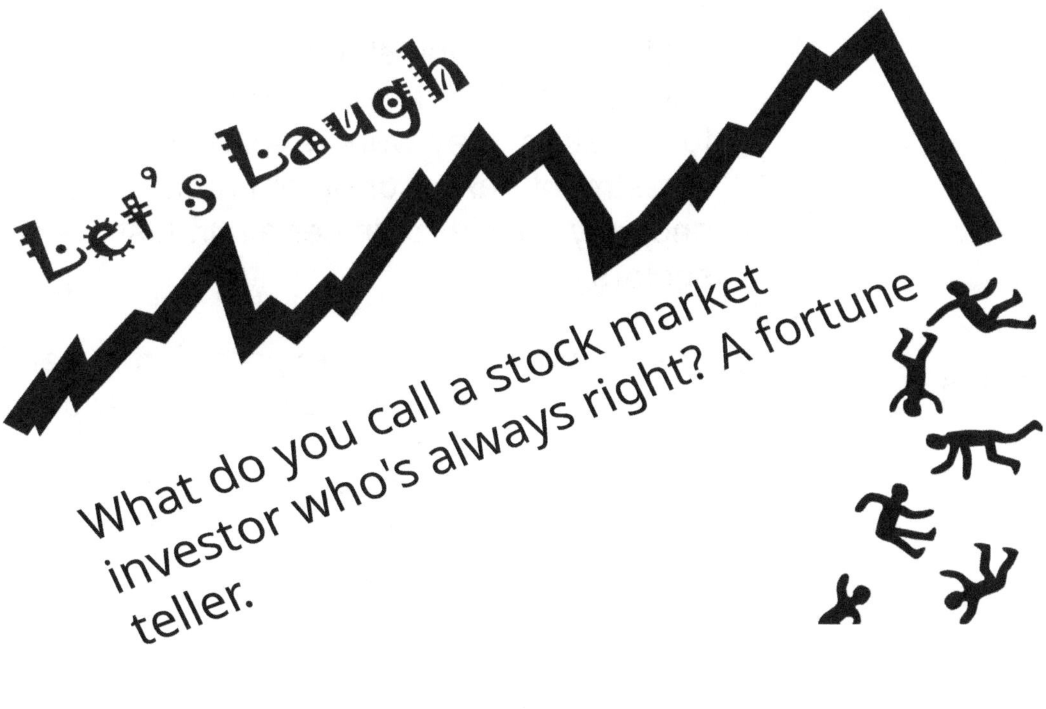


*See Solution on p. 175*

# Definition Match-Up #2

The 7 Participants in the Stock Market

**Associate the 7 Participants in the Stock Market to their Definitions:**

| | | | |
|---|---|---|---|
| **1** | Exchanges | **A** | Financial institutions or individuals that stand ready to buy or sell securities at any time, providing liquidity to markets. |
| **2** | Market makers | **B** | Agencies or organizations that oversee and regulate financial markets. Examples include SEC and FCA. |
| **3** | Regulators | **C** | Marketplaces where securities are bought and sold. Examples include NYSE, NASDAQ, and TSE. |
| **4** | Brokerages | **D** | Financial firms that help clients buy and sell securities. Can be full-service or discount. |
| **5** | Investors | **E** | Professionals who study and evaluate financial and economic data to make recommendations to investors. May work for brokerages, investment banks, or other financial institutions and may specialize in certain industries or sectors. |
| **6** | Companies | **F** | Buy securities with the expectation of earning a return. May seek income or capital appreciation. |
| **7** | Analysts | **G** | Legal entities that engage in business activities. Can be publicly traded (must disclose certain financial info) or privately held. |

*See Solution on p. 175*

# Cloze Test #2

## Fill In the Blanks Using the 7 Participants in the Stock market

| a) investors - b) analysts - c) Brokerages - d) Exchanges - e) Regulators - f) Market makers - g) Companies |
|---|

_______ listed on _______ around the world rely on a variety of different players to help them achieve success in the financial markets. Shareholders, for example, provide the capital that companies need to fund their operations and grow their businesses. Without the support of financiers, many companies would struggle to survive. _______, on the other hand, facilitate the buying and selling of stocks on behalf of their clients, helping to ensure that there is always liquidity in the market. Marketplaces, such as the New York Stock Exchange and the NASDAQ, provide the platforms on which stocks are traded and listed. _______, including the Securities and Exchange Commission (SEC) in the United States, are responsible for overseeing and regulating the financial markets to ensure that they operate fairly and transparently. _______, who are usually large financial institutions, also play a crucial role in the financial markets by providing liquidity and helping to match buyers and sellers. Finally, _______, who may be employed by trading firms or other financial firms, provide research and recommendations to help _______ make informed decisions about which stocks to buy or sell. Overall, the interactions between these various players help to create a healthy and functioning financial market.

*See Solution on p. 175*

# Missing Vowel #2

## Learn about the 7 participants in the Stock Market

| Word | Clue |
|---|---|
| _ X C H _ N G _ S | platforms where stocks and other securities are traded and listed |
| M _ R K _ T   M _ K _ R S | they facilitate the buying and selling of securities by providing liquidity to the market |
| R _ G _ L _ T _ R S | they oversee and regulate financial markets to ensure fair and transparent operations |
| C _ M P _ N _ _ S | they issue stocks and are listed on exchanges |
| _ N V _ S T _ R S | they buy and sell stocks |
| B R _ K _ R _ G _ S | they facilitate the buying and selling of stocks on behalf of clients |
| _ N _ L Y S T S | they study and provide research on stocks and other securities |

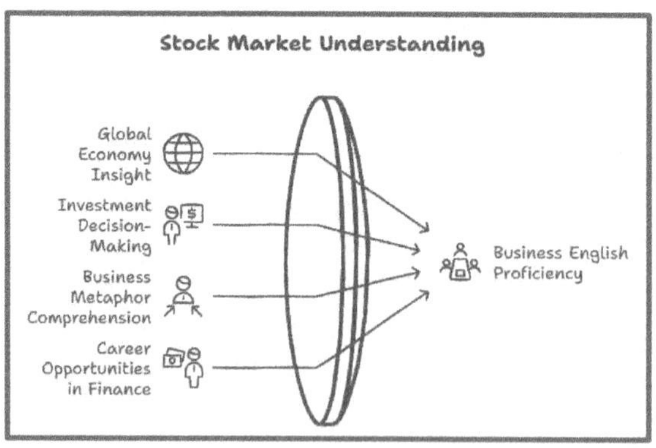


*See Solution on p. 176*

# Double Puzzle #2

## A list of words that describe the 7 Participants in the Stock Market

| Scrambled word | Box numbers |
|---|---|
| ALSYATNS | 69, 17, 65, 87, 7, _, 24, _ |
| IROVENTSS | 9, 40, _, 6, _, 1, 13, 64, _ |
| CNIEPMAOS | 32, 83, 75, 68, 59, 60, 16, 42, 10 |
| BOEEARKRGS | _, 27, 30, 5, 23, 14, 54, 18, 48, _ |
| MREAKT MREAKS | _, 76, 33, 78, 37, 29 / _, 39, 15, 71, 77, 67 |
| EANGCEXHS | 3, _, 46, 2, 35, 49, _, 34, _ |
| RTOGELURAS | 56, 26, 22, _, 88, 86, 20, 21, 70, _ |

_ _ _ (1 2 3) _ _ _ (5 6 7) _ _ (9 10) W _ _ _ _ _ _ (12 13 14 15 16 17 18) _ _ _ _ _ H _ _ (20 21 22 23 24 25 26 27)

_ _ (29 30) _ _ _ _ T _ (32 33 34 35 36 37) _ _ (39 40) _ F F I _ I _ _ T , (42 43 44 45 46 47 48 49 50 51)

F _ I _ , (53 54 55 56 57) _ _ D (59 60 61) T _ _ N _ _ _ _ _ N T (63 64 65 66 67 68 69 70 71 72 73)

_ _ _ _ E T (75 76 77 78 79 80) F _ R (82 83 84) _ _ _ . (86 87 88 89)

See Solution on p. 176

## Cryptogram #2 - The 7 Participants in the Stock Market

| A | B | C | D | E | F | G | H | I | J | K | L | M | N | O | P | Q | R | S | T | U | V | W | X | Y | Z |
|---|---|---|---|---|---|---|---|---|---|---|---|---|---|---|---|---|---|---|---|---|---|---|---|---|---|
| | | | | | | | | | | | | | | | | | | | | | | | | | |

W A H K O A R N O J    R Y G    G O R L O A J    V J O

J F O T E R L E Z O G    J H P X Q R A O    R Y G

R L N H A E X S U J    X H    O B O T V X O

X A R G O J    R X    L E N S X Y E Y N    J F O O G J

J H U O X E U O J    T H U F L O X E Y N    R

X A R G O    E Y    L O J J    X S R Y    R

U E L L E J O T H Y G

*See Solution on p. 176*

# Related Words  Matching #2

## Associate the Sectors of the Economy to their Related Words:

| 1 | Analysts | A | business, corporation, firm, enterprise, organization |
|---|---|---|---|
| 2 | Regulators | B | shareholders, stockholders, creditors, financiers, backers |
| 3 | Companies | C | firms, houses, agencies, dealerships, bureaus |
| 4 | Brokerages | D | markets, platforms, bourses, venues, boards |
| 5 | Market makers | E | authorities, overseers, controllers, monitors, supervisors |
| 6 | Exchanges | F | dealers, brokers, liquidity providers, underwriters, jobbers |
| 7 | Investors | G | researchers, experts, commentators, consultants, advisers |

*See Solution on p. 176*

**The 7 Participants in the Stock Market**

The stock market is a complex network of relationships and interactions among seven main participants: companies, investors, brokers, dealers, analysts, regulators, and market makers. Companies issue stocks to raise capital and fund business operations. Investors buy and sell stocks to generate profits or to fund long-term financial goals. Brokerages facilitate the buying and selling of stocks on behalf of investors. Dealers, also known as market makers, help to provide liquidity to the market by buying and selling stocks to other investors. Analysts provide research and analysis to help investors make informed decisions about buying and selling stocks. Regulators oversee the stock market to ensure that it operates fairly and transparently. Exchanges, such as the NYSE and NASDAQ, provide a platform for buying and selling stocks. All of these participants play a vital role in the functioning of the stock market and work together to create an efficient, fair, and transparent market for all.

# Multiple-Choice Quiz #2: Circle the Correct Answer

| | |
|---|---|
| 1. **Who issues stocks to raise capital and fund business operations?**<br><br>a. Investors<br>b. Brokerages<br>c. Regulators<br>d. Companies | 2. **Who buys and sells stocks to generate profits or fund long-term financial goals?**<br><br>a. Brokerages<br>b. Regulators<br>c. Companies<br>d. Investors |
| 3. **Who facilitates the buying and selling of stocks on behalf of investors?**<br><br>a. Market makers<br>b. Companies<br>c. Brokerages<br>d. Analysts | 4. **Who helps to provide liquidity to the market by buying and selling stocks to other investors?**<br><br>a. Companies<br>b. Brokerages<br>c. Market makers<br>d. Exchanges |

### The 7 Participants in the Stock Market

The stock market is a complex network of relationships and interactions among seven main participants: companies, investors, brokers, dealers, analysts, regulators, and market makers. Companies issue stocks to raise capital and fund business operations. Investors buy and sell stocks to generate profits or to fund long-term financial goals. Brokerages facilitate the buying and selling of stocks on behalf of investors. Dealers, also known as market makers, help to provide liquidity to the market by buying and selling stocks to other investors. Analysts provide research and analysis to help investors make informed decisions about buying and selling stocks. Regulators oversee the stock market to ensure that it operates fairly and transparently. Exchanges, such as the NYSE and NASDAQ, provide a platform for buying and selling stocks. All of these participants play a vital role in the functioning of the stock market and work together to create an efficient, fair, and transparent market for all.

## Multiple-Choice Quiz #2: Circle the Correct Answer

5. **Who provides research and analysis to help investors make informed decisions about buying and selling stocks?**

a. Regulators
b. Market makers
c. Analysts
d. Investors

6. **Who oversees the stock market to ensure that it operates fairly and transparently?**

a. Companies
b. Brokerages
c. Analysts
d. Regulators

7. **What provides a platform for buying and selling stocks?**

a. Investors
b. Market makers
c. Exchanges
d. Regulators

8. **What are dealers also known as?**

a. Brokers
b. Market makers
c. Companies
d. Regulators

9. **What are the NYSE and NASDAQ examples of?**

a. Brokerages
b. Market makers
c. Exchanges
d. Regulators

10. **Who plays a vital role in the functioning of the stock market and works together to create an efficient, fair, and transparent market for all?**

a. Companies
b. Investors
c. Brokerages
d. All of the above

*See Solution on p. 177*

# Trading Instruments: Securities and Commodities

As we delve deeper into the stock market jargon, it is important to first understand the distinction between various trading instruments and types of stocks.

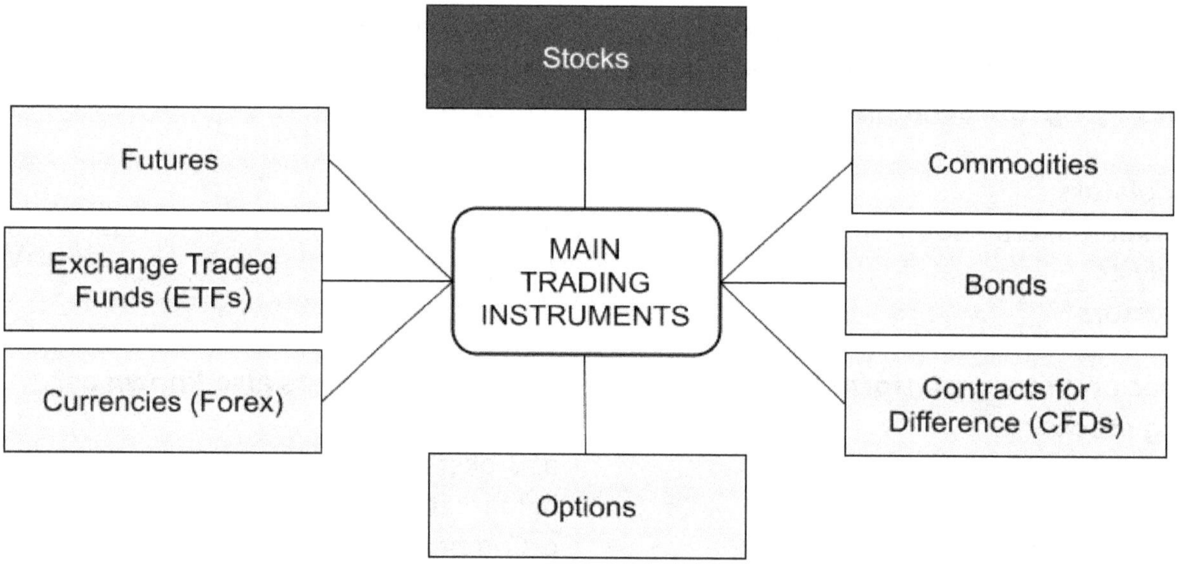


**What is a stock**?

As shown above, stocks are not the only thing that can be traded on the stock market. Stocks, also known as equities or shares, represent ownership in a company. When you own stocks in a company, you are a shareholder and are entitled to a portion of the company's profits and assets. Stocks are typically bought and sold through a stock exchange, such as the New York Stock Exchange (NYSE) or the NASDAQ.

# Trading Instruments: Securities and Commodities

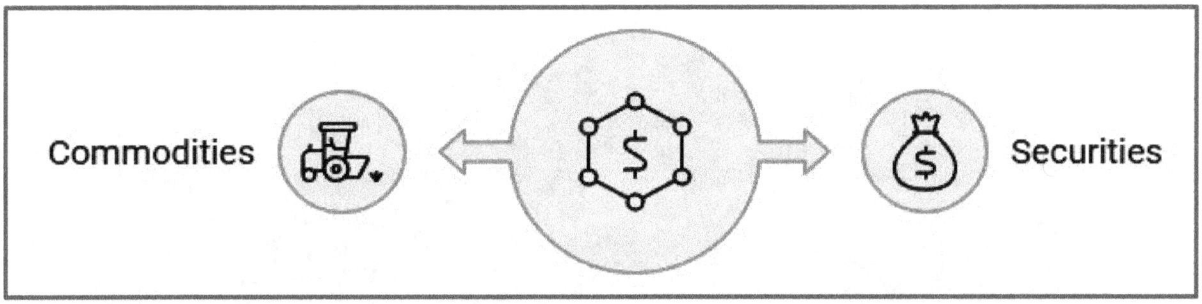


The value of a stock is determined by the supply and demand for the stock on the market. If more people want to buy a particular stock than sell it, the price of the stock will tend to rise. Conversely, if more people want to sell a particular stock than buy it, the price of the stock will tend to fall.

Before looking into the different types of stocks, we need to understand the difference between securities and commodities, keeping in mind that stocks are but one type of securities.

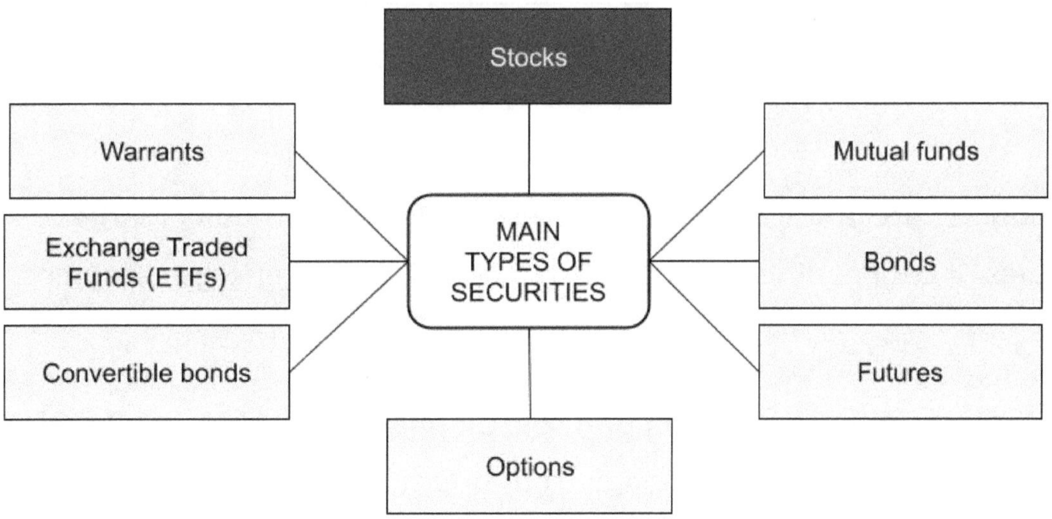


Securities are financial instruments that represent ownership in a company or a debt owed by a company or government. Examples of securities include stocks, bonds, and options.

# Trading Instruments: Securities and Commodities

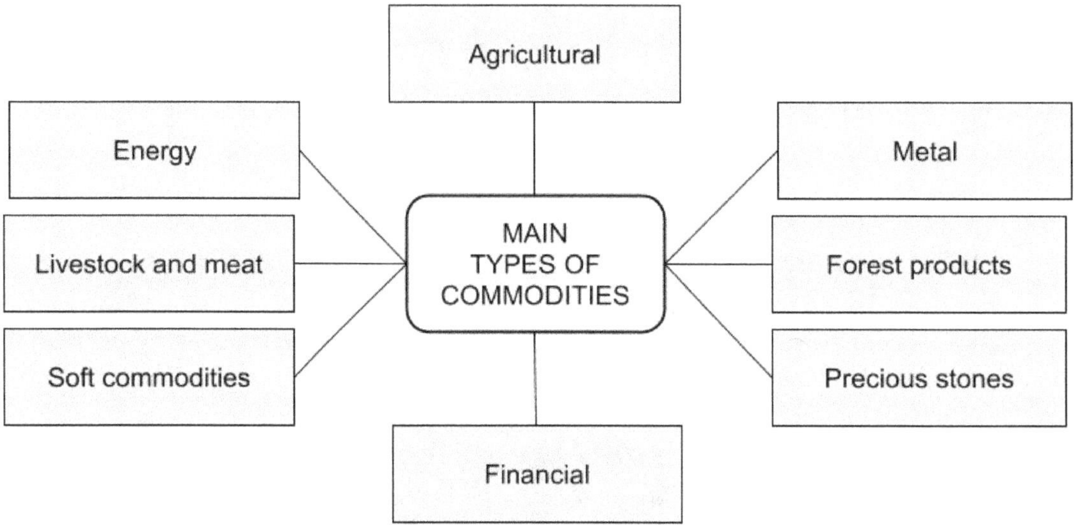


Commodities are physical goods that are traded on commodity markets. Examples of commodities include agricultural products, energy resources, and metals.

In general, securities are bought and sold on financial markets, while commodities are bought and sold on commodity markets. Securities represent a financial claim on an asset, while commodities are the actual physical assets being traded.

# Trading Instruments: Securities and Commodities

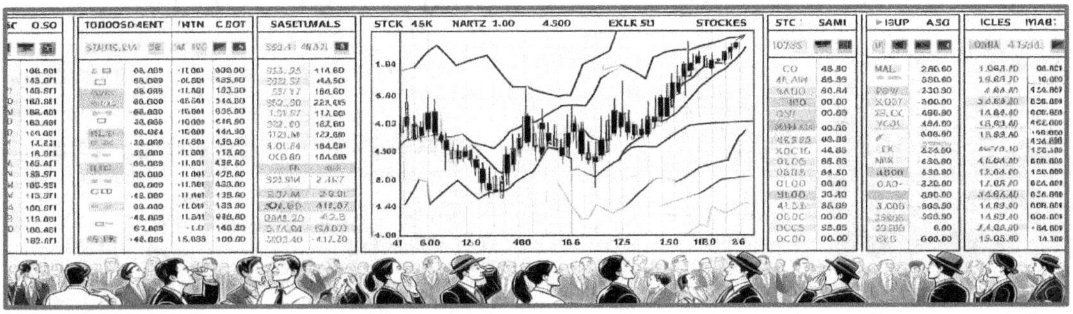

Now that we understand the distinction between securities, which are financial assets, and commodities, which are physical assets, we can examine different types of stock.

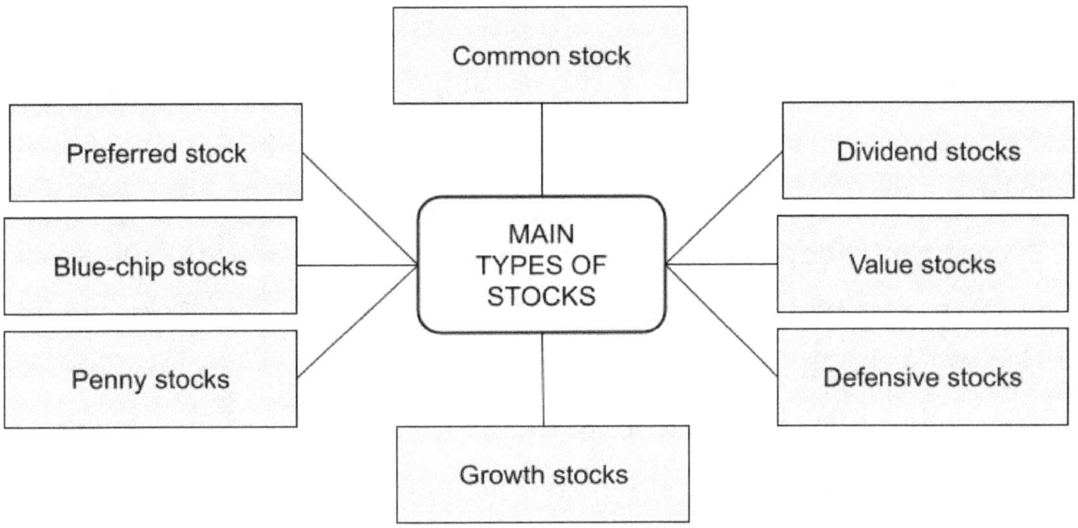


## Did You Know?

Stock and equity are often used interchangeably to refer to ownership interests in a company, but they can have slightly different meanings.
Stock refers to ownership shares in a company.
Equity refers to the value of an ownership interest in a company. It can refer to the total value of a company's stock, or it can refer to the amount of ownership that an individual or entity holds in a company. For example, if a company has $100,000 in assets and $50,000 in liabilities, the equity in the company would be $50,000.

# Trading Instruments: Securities and Commodities

## Main Trading Instruments: Definitions

1. **Stocks**: Stocks represent ownership in a company and are usually bought and sold through a stock exchange.
2. **Options**: Options are contracts that give the holder the right, but not the obligation, to buy or sell a specific asset at a specific price on or before a certain date.
3. **Futures**: Futures are contracts that obligate the buyer to purchase an asset, or the seller to sell an asset, at a specific price on a specific future date.
4. **Exchange-traded funds (ETFs)**: ETFs are investment funds that track the performance of a particular market index or asset class. They can be bought and sold like stocks.
5. **Currencies (Forex)**: The foreign exchange market (forex) is a global decentralized market for the trading of currencies.
6. **Commodities**: Commodities are raw materials or agricultural products that can be bought and sold, such as gold, oil, and wheat.
7. **Bonds**: Debt securities that represent a loan to a government, municipality, or corporation. Investors receive fixed interest payments and the return of principal when the bond matures. Risks include default and rising interest rates.
8. **CFDs (Contract for Difference)**: Financial derivatives that allow traders to speculate on the price movement of an underlying asset without owning the asset. They are leveraged products that are traded through brokers or financial institutions.

# Trading Instruments: Securities and Commodities

## Main Types of Securities: Definitions

1. **Stocks**: represent ownership in a company and entitle the holder to a share of the company's profits and assets.
2. **Bonds**: represent debt and are issued by governments and corporations as a way to raise capital. Investors lend money to the issuer in exchange for periodic interest payments and the return of principal when the bond matures.
3. **Options**: contracts that give the holder the right, but not the obligation, to buy or sell a security at a predetermined price within a specific time period.
4. **Futures**: contracts that obligate the buyer to purchase a security or commodity at a predetermined price at a specific time in the future.
5. **Mutual funds**: a type of investment vehicle that holds a diverse portfolio of stocks, bonds, or other securities and is managed by a professional investment company.
6. **Exchange-traded funds (ETFs)**: a type of investment vehicle that holds a diverse portfolio of stocks, bonds, or other securities and is traded on a stock exchange.
7. **Warrants**: securities that give the holder the right to purchase a specific number of shares of a company's stock at a predetermined price within a specific time period.
8. **Convertible bonds**: bonds that can be converted into a predetermined number of shares of the issuer's common stock at the holder's discretion.

# Trading Instruments: Securities and Commodities

## Main Types of Commodities: Definitions

1. **Agricultural commodities**: products produced by farming, such as wheat, corn, soybeans, and rice.
2. **Energy commodities**: resources used to produce energy, such as crude oil, natural gas, and coal.
3. **Metal commodities**: raw materials used in the production of goods, such as gold, silver, copper, and iron.
4. **Livestock and meat commodities**: animals raised for meat, such as cattle, pork, and chicken.
5. **Soft commodities**: agricultural products that are grown in tropical or subtropical climates, such as coffee, cocoa, and sugar.
6. **Forest products**: raw materials derived from forests, such as timber and pulp.
7. **Precious stones**: rare and valuable stones, such as diamonds, emeralds, and rubies.
8. **Financial commodities**: financial instruments that are traded on commodity markets, such as currencies and futures contracts.

# Trading Instruments: Securities and Commodities

## Main Types of Stocks: Definitions

1. **Common stock**: represents ownership in a company and entitles the holder to a share of the company's profits and assets. Common shareholders have voting rights and may be able to participate in the company's management.
2. **Preferred stock**: a type of stock that has a higher claim on the company's assets and earnings than common stock. Preferred shareholders generally do not have voting rights, but they may receive a fixed dividend.
3. **Blue-chip stocks**: stocks of well-established companies with a strong track record of performance and stability.
4. **Penny stocks**: stocks that are priced at less than $5 per share and are considered to be high-risk investments.
5. **Growth stocks**: stocks of companies that are expected to experience rapid growth and generate high returns for shareholders.
6. **Value stocks**: stocks of companies that are believed to be undervalued by the market and have the potential to generate high returns.
7. **Dividend stocks**: stocks that pay dividends to shareholders and are typically less risky than growth stocks.
8. **Defensive stocks**: stocks of companies that are less vulnerable to economic downturns and tend to perform well in times of market volatility.

## Word Search Puzzle #3a - Trading Instruments (securities and equities)

Find the Trading Instruments in the list below

| | | | | | | | | | | | | | | | |
|---|---|---|---|---|---|---|---|---|---|---|---|---|---|---|---|
| O | F | K | R | Q | R | B | U | H | F | U | J | N | R | N | X |
| B | V | R | B | C | U | R | R | E | N | C | I | E | S | H | F |
| W | L | C | O | M | M | O | D | I | T | I | E | S | U | V | P |
| A | A | C | F | D | S | O | Q | N | D | D | A | Z | J | G | Y |
| E | G | W | K | L | V | Z | R | O | O | W | P | H | V | F | S |
| J | L | O | W | G | J | A | J | N | O | W | L | P | C | Y | F |
| S | G | C | N | P | S | F | T | E | C | P | X | M | D | L | U |
| M | T | I | H | D | W | S | D | R | I | S | T | W | C | J | M |
| G | E | O | X | P | S | E | R | U | T | U | F | I | D | B | M |
| K | Z | R | C | P | A | B | C | S | F | N | R | E | O | A | H |
| A | A | C | X | K | E | R | F | S | N | A | U | N | C | N | O |
| Q | C | B | L | T | S | C | E | S | I | K | D | W | I | Q | S |
| D | G | I | E | C | P | P | U | E | V | S | A | R | E | F | W |
| R | Q | P | B | P | S | D | D | Q | Z | M | W | H | X | J | Z |
| A | Y | Z | U | J | Q | L | J | D | A | Z | U | I | W | Y | V |
| M | Z | P | G | O | H | C | B | O | H | K | W | R | D | V | U |

BONDS
COMMODITIES
ETFS
OPTIONS
CFDS
CURRENCIES
FUTURES
STOCKS

*See Solution on p. 177*

## Word Search Puzzle #3b - Trading Instruments (securities and equities)

Find the Types of Securities in the list below

| | | | | | | | | | | | | | | | |
|---|---|---|---|---|---|---|---|---|---|---|---|---|---|---|---|
| W | S | A | G | D | Z | B | R | X | Q | C | H | X | T | C | S |
| H | C | K | N | W | H | S | M | P | G | E | Q | M | E | O | T |
| D | O | L | F | T | K | I | J | W | L | X | B | F | L | N | N |
| C | I | R | E | C | V | B | B | B | Y | F | C | D | L | V | A |
| M | P | Y | O | K | W | X | C | C | G | C | G | K | M | E | R |
| E | C | T | N | M | K | C | X | V | S | A | G | S | U | R | R |
| Q | S | S | C | Y | F | M | H | B | N | A | A | N | T | T | A |
| E | Y | C | Y | S | H | U | Z | X | B | W | S | O | U | I | W |
| T | N | P | W | Q | U | A | T | Y | P | U | R | I | A | B | K |
| Y | O | P | N | O | X | B | Q | U | J | E | H | T | L | L | X |
| H | E | J | S | I | Y | E | O | W | R | K | I | P | F | E | A |
| O | U | T | L | D | W | T | A | N | O | E | T | O | U | B | H |
| H | Q | Y | X | Z | V | F | N | I | D | Z | S | O | N | O | V |
| M | X | V | D | H | Q | S | I | E | L | S | I | Y | D | N | E |
| P | U | P | V | T | S | J | K | A | E | T | N | P | S | D | Q |
| A | K | F | E | V | K | E | L | F | Y | B | S | U | O | S | L |

BONDS
ETFS
MUTUAL FUNDS
STOCKS

CONVERTIBLE BONDS
FUTURES
OPTIONS
WARRANTS

*See Solution on p. 177*

## Word Search Puzzle #3c - Trading Instruments (securities and equities)

Find the Types of Commodities in the list below

| | | | | | | | | | | | | | | | |
|---|---|---|---|---|---|---|---|---|---|---|---|---|---|---|---|
| P | S | X | T | D | X | C | H | V | B | T | M | P | A | F | I |
| S | E | I | T | I | D | O | M | M | O | C | T | F | O | S | H |
| V | F | U | M | T | U | S | Y | V | Y | E | A | H | E | K | K |
| K | N | P | I | X | E | N | C | B | U | Z | Q | E | I | M | T |
| Z | K | X | G | Q | A | U | K | S | H | P | G | L | H | V | S |
| A | S | F | O | R | E | S | T | P | R | O | D | U | C | T | S |
| V | S | A | G | R | I | C | U | L | T | U | R | E | K | E | P |
| C | N | U | U | F | B | H | V | B | F | E | V | P | L | R | I |
| E | I | D | G | Y | E | H | O | N | M | U | C | Q | D | E | A |
| W | X | W | P | Z | Q | H | U | E | H | G | E | V | N | A | L |
| X | E | V | D | I | Z | O | T | W | H | A | Y | E | W | A | Y |
| U | Q | E | K | B | T | A | O | G | I | C | R | B | X | T | Y |
| B | S | I | X | K | L | F | T | E | R | G | V | A | V | O | Y |
| Y | R | I | L | D | R | X | X | N | Y | F | D | Q | M | F | U |
| H | W | S | E | N | O | T | S | S | U | O | I | C | E | R | P |
| L | I | V | E | S | T | O | C | K | A | N | D | M | E | A | T |

AGRICULTURE
FOREST PRODUCTS
METAL
SOFT COMMODITIES
ENERGY
LIVESTOCK AND MEAT
PRECIOUS STONES

*See Solution on p. 177*

## Word Search Puzzle #3d - Trading Instruments (securities and equities)

Find the Types of Stocks in the list below

| | | | | | | | | | | | | | | | |
|---|---|---|---|---|---|---|---|---|---|---|---|---|---|---|---|
| P | E | P | M | H | L | R | I | Q | M | C | S | G | W | P | D |
| X | Z | G | J | P | R | H | T | I | P | K | F | G | R | V | E |
| U | S | L | P | A | M | R | U | I | C | B | R | E | A | D | F |
| V | M | Y | X | D | C | K | H | O | B | O | F | L | D | I | E |
| Q | U | J | U | V | B | C | T | E | W | E | U | P | Z | V | N |
| E | O | C | X | J | E | S | E | T | R | E | W | E | M | I | S |
| F | W | F | F | U | N | Q | H | R | S | P | H | N | M | D | I |
| B | O | Q | L | O | G | S | E | T | G | W | X | N | K | E | V |
| J | N | B | M | D | T | D | O | E | M | C | X | Y | B | N | E |
| O | V | M | Y | O | S | C | U | A | W | L | Y | S | I | D | S |
| W | O | I | C | T | K | Z | C | K | U | W | E | T | O | S | T |
| C | A | K | O | S | E | G | X | F | I | T | A | O | L | T | O |
| M | S | C | X | Y | G | Y | G | K | A | D | V | C | B | O | C |
| Z | K | L | K | P | F | K | I | D | I | F | G | K | R | C | K |
| A | S | U | X | J | R | N | D | E | N | K | D | S | M | K | S |
| F | I | B | Y | S | G | G | M | I | B | C | Q | L | F | S | G |

BLUE-CHIP
DEFENSIVE STOCKS
GROWTH STOCKS
PREFERRED STOCK
COMMON STOCKS
DIVIDEND STOCKS
PENNY STOCKS
VALUE STOCKS

*See Solution on p. 178*

# Crossword Puzzle #3a - Trading Instruments

## Learn about Trading Instruments

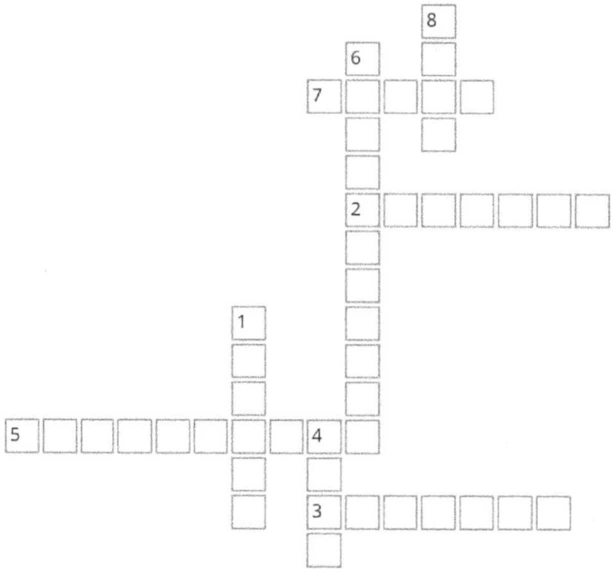

Across

**[2]** Contracts that give the holder the right (but not the obligation) to buy or sell a financial instrument at a predetermined price.

**[3]** Contracts that obligate the buyer to purchase a financial instrument at a predetermined price at a future date.

**[5]** Forms of money issued by governments or central banks, such as the US dollar or the euro.

**[7]** Debt securities issued by governments, municipalities, or corporations.

Down

**[1]** Securities that represent ownership in a company.

**[4]** Investment funds that track the performance of a specific market index or asset class.

**[6]** Raw materials or agricultural products that are traded on financial markets.

**[8]** Contracts for difference, which are financial instruments that allow traders to speculate on the price movements of underlying assets without actually owning them.

*See Solution on p. 178*

# Crossword Puzzle #3b - Trading Instruments

## Learn about Types of Securities

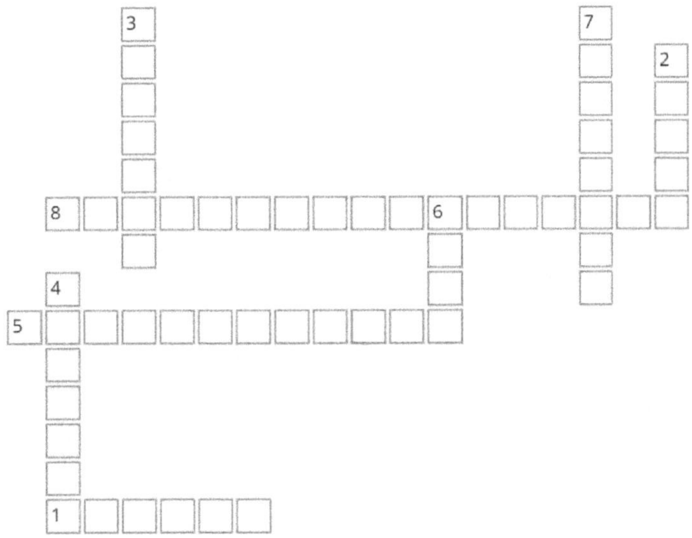


Across

**[1]** Securities that represent ownership in a company.

**[5]** Investment vehicles that pool together the money of many investors and use it to buy a diversified portfolio of stocks, bonds, or other securities.

**[8]** Bonds that can be exchanged for a specified number of shares of the issuing company's stock at a predetermined price.

Down

**[2]** Debt securities issued by governments, municipalities, or corporations.

**[3]** Contracts that give the holder the right (but not the obligation) to buy or sell a financial instrument at a predetermined price.

**[4]** Contracts that obligate the buyer to purchase a financial instrument at a predetermined price at a future date.

**[6]** Investment funds that track the performance of a specific market index or asset class.

**[7]** Securities that give the holder the right to buy a certain number of shares of stock at a predetermined price for a specific period of time.

*See Solution on p. 178*

# Crossword Puzzle #3c - Trading Instruments

## Learn about Types of Commodities

Across

**[4]** Animals such as cows, pigs, and chickens that are raised for their meat, milk, or eggs.

**[5]** Agricultural products such as grains, oil seeds, and fibers.

**[7]** Valuable gems such as diamonds, emeralds, and rubies that are prized for their beauty and rarity.

**[8]** Financial instruments such as futures, options, and swaps used to speculate on or hedge against price movements.

Down

**[1]** The production of crops, livestock, and other related products.

**[2]** Resources such as oil, natural gas, and coal that are used to generate electricity and power transportation.

**[3]** A class of elements that are characterized by their high conductivity of electricity and heat and their malleability and ductility.

**[6]** Raw materials such as timber, pulp, and paper that are derived from forests.

*See Solution on p. 178*

# Crossword Puzzle #3d - Trading Instruments

## Learn about Types of Stocks

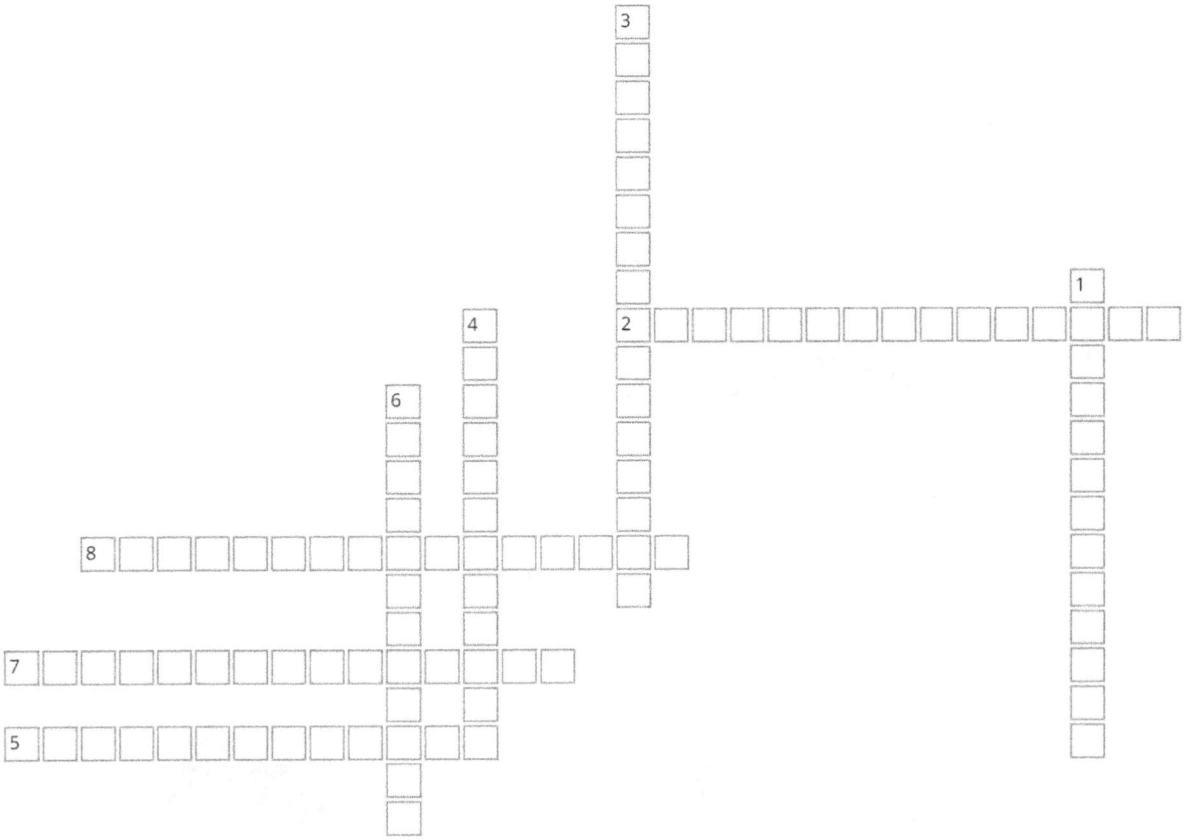


Across

**[2]** Give the holder priority over common shareholders in terms of dividend payments and in the event of the company's liquidation.

**[5]** Are expected to grow at a faster rate than the market as a whole.

**[7]** Pay regular payouts to their shareholders.

**[8]** Are expected to perform well during times of economic uncertainty or market volatility.

Down

**[1]** Represent ownership in a company and entitle the holder to vote at shareholder meetings and receive dividends.

**[3]** The stocks of well-established, financially sound companies with a long track record of stability and strong performance.

**[4]** Priced at less than $5 per share and are typically issued by small, speculative companies.

**[6]** Are believed to be undervalued relative to their intrinsic worth.

*See Solution on p. 179*

## Scramble Puzzle #3a - Trading Instruments

Uncramble the Trading Instruments in the list below

CNREERIUCS

CEMOTIOMDIS

ODSNB

SKCTOS

FEST

OTINPOS

SDCF

FTREUUS

*See Solution on p. 179*

## Scramble Puzzle #3b - Trading Instruments

**Uncramble the Types of Securities in the list below**

NBSOD ☐☐☐☐☐

CELITBRNVOE NSDOB ☐☐☐☐☐☐☐☐☐☐☐ ☐☐☐☐☐

FEST ☐☐☐☐

FTEUURS ☐☐☐☐☐☐☐

MAUTUL DSUNF ☐☐☐☐☐☐ ☐☐☐☐☐

ONPTIOS ☐☐☐☐☐☐☐

SCTKOS ☐☐☐☐☐☐

WTNRAARS ☐☐☐☐☐☐☐☐

*See Solution on p. 179*

## Scramble Puzzle #3c - Trading Instruments

Uncramble the Types of Commodities in the list below

FANNIAICL CDIEOIMOMTS

PURECIOS SNTEOS

FSORET PDRUCTOS

TSOF CMOEDITMIOS

LVETCOSIK DAN EATM

ELMTA

ARIRUGULTCE

EGRNEY

*See Solution on p.179*

## Scramble Puzzle #3d - Trading Instruments

**Uncramble the Types of Stocks in the list below**

| Scrambled | Answer |
|---|---|
| DFEIENVSE SKCTOS | |
| DNIEIVDD SKCTOS | |
| UEVAL SKTOCS | |
| GOTRWH SKCTOS | |
| YNPEN SOCKTS | |
| BUECLI-HP SKCTOS | |
| PERERFRED COSKT | |
| CMOMON SKTOCS | |

Why did the stock trader switch from trading stocks to trading surgical instruments? Because he wanted to make some real cuts in the market!

*See Solution on p. 180*

# Definition Match-Up #3a

Trading Instruments (securities and commodities)

## Associate the *Trading Instruments* in the Stock Market to their Definitions

| | | | |
|---|---|---|---|
| **1** | Stocks | **A** | Securities that represent an ownership interest in a company. They can be bought and sold on a stock exchange. |
| **2** | Options | **B** | Financial instruments that give the holder the right, but not the obligation, to buy or sell an underlying asset at a predetermined price within a certain time frame. |
| **3** | Futures | **C** | Contracts that obligate the buyer to purchase an asset, or the seller to sell an asset, at a predetermined price at a specified time in the future. |
| **4** | ETFs | **D** | Investment funds that are traded on stock exchanges and track an underlying index, a commodity, or a basket of assets. |
| **5** | Currencies | **E** | forms of money that are used in different countries around the world. They can be traded in the foreign exchange market. |
| **6** | Commodities | **F** | Physical goods that are traded on commodity exchanges, such as agricultural products, energy products, and metal products. |
| **7** | Bonds | **G** | Debt securities that are issued by governments and corporations to raise capital. They pay periodic interest to the bondholder and return the principal when the bond matures. |
| **8** | CFDs | **H** | Financial instruments that allow traders to speculate on the price movements of an underlying asset without actually owning it. |

*See Solution on p. 180*

# Definition Match-Up #3b

## Trading Instruments (securities and commodities)

### Associate the *Types of Securities* in the Stock Market to their Definitions

| | | | |
|---|---|---|---|
| **1** | Warrants | **A** | Financial derivatives that give the holder the right, but not the obligation, to buy or sell an underlying asset at a predetermined price on or before a specified date. |
| **2** | Stocks | **B** | Investment vehicles that pool together money from many investors and use it to buy a diversified portfolio of stocks, bonds, or other securities. |
| **3** | Convertible bonds | **C** | Mutual funds that trade on a stock exchange like a stock. |
| **4** | Bonds | **D** | Contracts that obligate the buyer to purchase an asset or the seller to sell an asset at a predetermined price on a specific future date. |
| **5** | Mutual funds | **E** | Financial instruments that give the holder the right to buy a specified number of shares at a predetermined price. |
| **6** | Options | **F** | A type of debt security that pay periodic interest to bondholders and return the principal when the bonds mature. They are issued by governments, municipalities, and corporations to raise capital. |
| **7** | Futures | **G** | Bonds that can be converted into a specified number of shares of the issuing company's stock. |
| **8** | ETFs | **H** | Also known as equities or shares. Represent ownership in a company. They allow shareholders to share in the company's profits and losses. |

*See Solution on p. 180*

# Definition Match-Up #3c

Trading Instruments (securities and commodities)

## Associate the *Types of Commodities* in the Stock Market to their Definitions

| | | | |
|---|---|---|---|
| **1** | Energy | **A** | Commodities such as coffee, cocoa, and cotton that are grown for their fibers or other usable parts. |
| **2** | Metal | **B** | Commodities such as grains, beans, fruits, and vegetables that are grown for human and animal consumption. |
| **3** | Agriculture | **C** | Commodities such as lumber, paper, and pulp that are derived from trees. |
| **4** | Livestock and meat | **D** | Commodities such as currencies, stocks, and bonds that are traded on financial markets. |
| **5** | Soft commodities | **E** | Commodities such as diamonds, emeralds, and rubies that are valued for their rarity and beauty. |
| **6** | Forest products | **F** | Commodities such as oil, natural gas, and electricity that are used to power homes, businesses, and industries. |
| **7** | Precious stones | **G** | Commodities such as cattle, pigs, and poultry that are raised for meat production. |
| **8** | Financial commodities | **H** | Commodities such as gold, silver, copper, and aluminum that are mined and used in various industries. |

*See Solution on p. 180*

# Definition Match-Up #3d

Trading Instruments (securities and commodities)

## Associate the *Types of Stocks* in the Stock Market to their Definitions

| | | | |
|---|---|---|---|
| **1** | Value stocks | **A** | Stocks of companies that are expected to grow faster than the overall market. |
| **2** | Blue-chip stocks | **B** | A type of stock that has a higher claim on a company's assets and earnings than common stock, but typically does not have voting rights. |
| **3** | Growth stocks | **C** | Stocks of small, low-priced companies that trade at less than $5 per share. |
| **4** | Dividend stocks | **D** | Stocks of companies that are undervalued by the market and offer a good risk-to-reward ratio. |
| **5** | Preferred stocks | **E** | Represents ownership in a company and entitles the holder to voting rights, dividends, and a share of the company's assets. |
| **6** | Defensive stocks | **F** | Stocks of companies that are less affected by economic downturns and tend to perform well in times of market volatility. |
| **7** | Penny stocks | **G** | Stocks of companies that pay out a portion of their profits to shareholders in the form of dividends. |
| **8** | Common stocks | **H** | Stocks of well-established, financially stable companies that have a long track record of steady growth. |

*See Solution on p. 181*

# Cloze Test #3a

## Fill In the Blanks Using the 8 Trading Instruments below:

| a) Stocks - b) Options - c) Futures - d) ETFs - e) Currencies - f) Commodities - g) Bonds - h) CFDs |
| --- |

There are many financial instruments available for trading in the stock market, not just _______. _______, or contracts for difference, are a type of financial instrument that allow traders to speculate on the price movement of an asset without actually owning it. _______ give the holder the right, but not the obligation, to buy or sell an underlying asset at a predetermined price. _______ are physical goods that are traded on financial markets, such as oil, gold, and wheat. _______, or exchange-traded funds, are investment funds that track the performance of a particular market or sector. _______ are debt instruments issued by governments and corporations to raise capital. _______ are financial instruments used to facilitate international trade and investment. _______ contracts are agreements to buy or sell a specific asset at a future date at a predetermined price.

*See Solution on p. 182*

# Cloze Test #3b

## Fill In the Blanks Using the 8 Types of Securities below:

a) Stocks - b) Bonds - c) Options - d) Futures - e) Mutual funds - f) ETFs - g) Warrants - h) Convertible

Keep in mind that there are many types of securities available for trading in the stock market, not just stocks. _______ contracts are agreements to buy or sell a specific asset at a future date at a predetermined price. _______ give the holder the right, but not the obligation, to buy or sell an underlying asset at a predetermined price. _______ bonds are bonds that can be converted into a specified number of shares of the issuing company's common stock. _______ are financial instruments that give the holder the right to purchase shares of the underlying stock at a predetermined price and at a specific time in the future. _______ are investment vehicles that pool together the money of multiple investors and use it to buy a diversified portfolio of stocks, bonds, or other securities. _______ are investment funds that track the performance of a particular market or sector. _______ are debt instruments issued by governments and corporations to raise capital.

*See Solution on p. 182*

# Cloze Test #3c

## Fill In the Blanks Using the 8 Types of Commodities below:

a) Livestock and meat - b) Forest products -
c) Soft commodities - d) Metal - e) Precious stones -
f) Energy - g) Agriculture - h) Financial commodities

There are many types of commodities available for trading in the stock market, not just securities. _______ include financial instruments such as currencies, bonds, and futures contracts. _______ includes physical goods such as grains, livestock, and other products related to farming. _______ and _______ includes physical goods such as cattle, pork, and poultry. _______ includes physical goods such as oil, natural gas, and coal. _______ include physical goods such as diamonds, gold, and other precious gems. _______ includes physical goods such as copper, aluminum, and steel. _______ include physical goods such as coffee, cocoa, and sugar. _______ products include physical goods such as lumber and paper.

*See Solution on p. 182*

# Cloze Test #3d

## Fill In the Blanks Using the 8 Types of Stocks below:

a) Common stocks - b) Preferred stocks - c) Blue-chip stocks - d) Penny stocks - e) Growth stocks - f) Value stocks - g) Dividend stocks - h) Defensive stocks

There are many types of stocks available for trading in the stock market. Understanding the differences between stock categories helps investors make better decisions and better manage risk within their portfolios. _______ are low-priced stocks that trade for less than $5 per share. _______ stocks are stocks that tend to perform well during times of economic downturn or market volatility. _______ stocks are stocks in companies that are expected to grow at an above-average rate compared to the overall market. _______ stocks are stocks in well-established and financially stable companies with a long track record of steady growth. _______ stocks are stocks that pay out a portion of their profits to shareholders in the form of dividends. _______ stocks are a type of hybrid security that combines features of both stocks and bonds. _______ stocks are the most widely known and traded type of stock, representing ownership in a company. _______ stocks are stocks in companies that are believed to be undervalued by the market.

*See Solution on p. 182*

## Missing Vowel #3a

### Learn about Trading Instruments in the Stock Market

| Word | Clue |
|---|---|
| C _ R R _ N C _ _ S | Forms of money issued by governments or central banks, such as the US dollar or the euro. |
| C _ M M _ D _ T _ _ S | Raw materials or agricultural products that are traded on financial markets. |
| B _ N D S | Debt securities issued by governments, municipalities, or corporations. |
| S T _ C K S | Securities that represent ownership in a company. |
| _ P T _ _ N S | Contracts that give the holder the right (but not the obligation) to buy or sell a financial instrument at a predetermined price. |
| F _ T _ R _ S | Contracts that obligate the buyer to purchase a financial instrument at a predetermined price at a future date. |
| _ T F S | Investment funds that track the performance of a specific market index or asset class. |
| C _ N T R _ C T S   F _ R   D _ F F _ R _ N C _ | Financial instruments that allow traders to speculate on the price movements of underlying assets without actually owning them. |

*See Solution on p. 183*

## Missing Vowel #3b

### Learn about Types of Securities in the Stock Market

| Word | Clue |
|---|---|
| M _ T _ _ L   F _ N D S | Investment vehicles that pool together the money of many investors and use it to buy a diversified portfolio. |
| C _ N V _ R T _ B L _   B _ N D S | Bonds that can be exchanged for a specified number of shares of the issuing company's stock at a predetermined price. |
| W _ R R _ N T S | Securities that give the holder the right to buy a certain number of shares of stock at a predetermined price for a specific period of time. |
| _ T F S | Investment funds that track the performance of a specific market index or asset class. |
| F _ T _ R _ S | Contracts that obligate the buyer to purchase a financial instrument at a predetermined price at a future date. |
| _ P T _ _ N S | Contracts that give the holder the right (but not the obligation) to buy or sell a financial instrument at a predetermined price. |
| B _ N D S | Debt securities issued by governments, municipalities, or corporations. |
| S T _ C K S | Securities that represent ownership in a company. |

*See Solution on p. 183*

## Missing Vowel #3c

### Learn about Types of Commodities in the Stock Market

| Puzzle | Clue |
|---|---|
| F _ N _ N C _ _ L   C _ M M _ D _ T _ _ S | Financial instruments such as futures, options, and swaps that are used to speculate on or hedge against price movements in underlying assets. |
| P R _ C _ _ _ S   S T _ N _ S | Valuable gems such as diamonds, emeralds, and rubies that are prized for their beauty and rarity. |
| F _ R _ S T   P R _ D _ C T S | Raw materials such as timber, pulp, and paper that are derived from forests. |
| S _ F T   C _ M M _ D _ T _ _ S | Agricultural products such as grains, oilseeds, and fibers that are grown and harvested for consumption or use in manufacturing. |
| L _ V _ S T _ C K   _ N D   M _ _ T | Animals such as cows, pigs, and chickens that are raised for their meat, milk, or eggs. |
| M _ T _ L | A class of elements that are characterized by their high conductivity of electricity and heat and their malleability and ductility. |
| _ N _ R G Y | Resources such as oil, natural gas, and coal that are used to generate electricity and power transportation. |

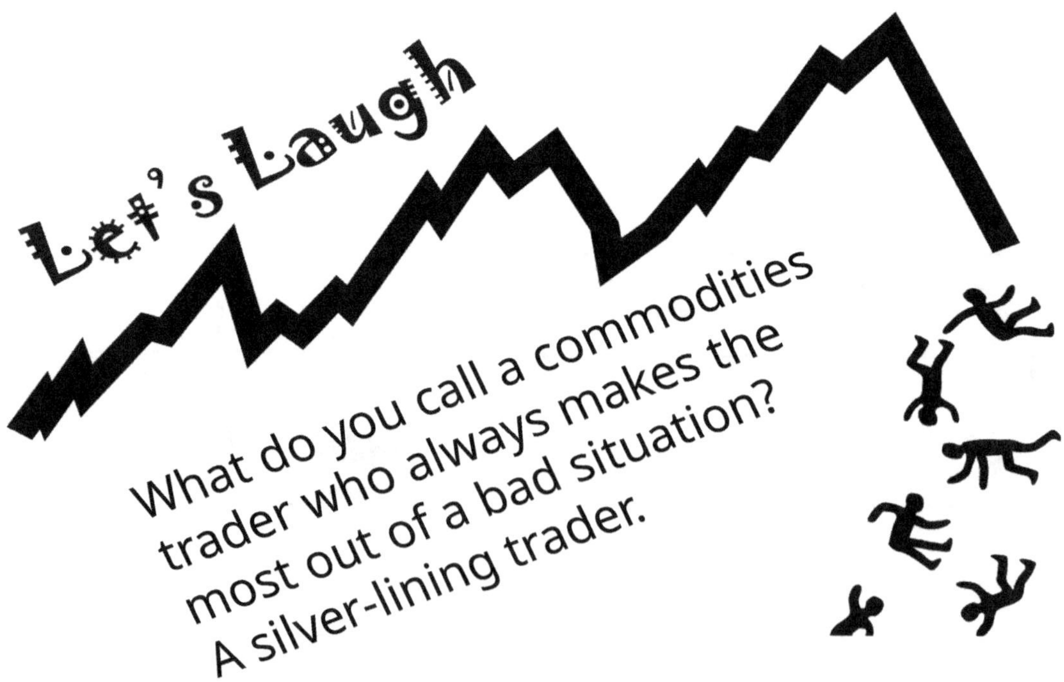


*See Solution on p. 183*

## Missing Vowel #3d

### Learn about Types of Stocks in the Stock Market

| Puzzle | Clue |
| --- | --- |
| P _ N N Y   S T _ C K S | Stocks that are priced at less than $1 per share and are typically issued by small, speculative companies. |
| G R _ W T H   S T _ C K S | Stocks of companies that are expected to grow at a faster rate than the market as a whole. |
| V _ L _ _   S T _ C K S | Stocks of companies that are believed to be undervalued relative to their intrinsic worth. |
| D _ F _ N S _ V _   S T _ C K S | Stocks of companies that are expected to perform well during times of economic uncertainty or market volatility. |
| D _ V _ D _ N D   S T _ C K S | Stocks that pay regular dividends to their shareholders. |
| B L _ _ - C H _ P   S T _ C K S | A term used to describe the stocks of well-established, financially sound companies with a long track record of stability and strong performance. |
| P R _ F _ R R _ D   S T _ C K | Securities that give the holder priority over common shareholders in terms of dividend payments and the right to receive assets in the event of the company's liquidation. |
| C _ M M _ N   S T _ C K S | Securities that represent ownership in a company and entitle the holder to vote at shareholder meetings and receive dividends. |

*See Solution on p. 183*

# Double Puzzle #3a

**A list of words that describe the Trading Instruments in the Stock Market**

| Scrambled word | Box numbers |
|---|---|
| SCTKOS | 47 14 22 _ 97 77 |
| OTNPIOS | 59 94 1 16 73 7 92 |
| FERUUTS | 60 23 12 6 38 3 11 |
| TFSE | 62 24 5 36 |
| CRICUEENRS | _ 39 27 74 10 17 _ 34 56 86 |
| CEMIMODOTIS | 88 134 40 72 75 29 9 26 30 41 111 |
| DSBON | 21 95 8 132 83 |
| DCSF | _ 105 115 44 |

_ H _   _ _ _ _ _ _ _ _   _ H _ _ G   A _ _ _ _   _ _ A _ _ N G
(1–3, 5–12, 14–18, 20–24, 26–32)

_ N _ T _ _ _ _ _ N T _   I _   T H A T   T H _ Y   _ _ T _ N
(34–44, 46–47, 49–52, 54–57, 59–63)

H A V E   H U _ _ _ _ U _   N A M E _ ,   _ U _ H   A _   _ _ R _
(65–68, 70–77, 79–84, 86–89, 91–92, 94–97)

B E L L Y   _ U T U R E _   A N _   B U T T E R F L Y   S P R E A _
(99–103, 105–111, 113–115, 117–125, 127–132)

_ P T I O N S .
(134–141)

*See Solution on p. 184*

# Double Puzzle #3b

A list of words that describe the Types of Securities in the Stock Market

SBOND _ _ _ _ _ (40 120 38)

CTONVBRELIE SBOND _ _ _ _ _ _ _ _ _ _ _ _ _ _ _ _ (3 70 20 2 47 31 6 57 24 16 116 60)

MAUUTL DFUSN _ _ _ _ _ _ _ _ _ _ _ (56 119 21 29 12 25 41 4 71)

WRARNTAS _ _ _ _ _ _ _ _ (49 44 5 59 23 68 51 10)

SFET _ _ _ _ (14 66 17)

OIONPTS _ _ _ _ _ _ _ (33 7 8 85 54)

SKTOCS _ _ _ _ _ _ (18 73 108 36 96 1)

FRUTEUS _ _ _ _ _ _ _ (115 55 65 13 9 30)

_ _ _ _ _ _ _ _ _ _ (1 2 3 4 5 6 7 8 9 10) _ _ _ (12 13 14) _ _ _ E _ _ I _ _ _ Y (16 17 18 19 20 21 22 23 24 25 26) J _ _ _ (28 29 30 31)

_ I E _ E _ (33 34 35 36 37 38) _ _ (40 41) P _ P E _ (43 44 45 46 47) _ I _ H (49 50 51 52) _ _ _ _ E _ _ (54 55 56 57 58 59 60)

W R I _ _ E _ (62 63 64 65 66 67 68) _ _ (70 71) _ H E M , (73 74 75 76 77) Y E T (79 80 81) P E _ P L E (83 84 85 86 87 88) A C T (90 91 92)

L I _ E (94 95 96 97) T H E Y ' R E (99 100 101 102 103 104 105) W _ R T H (107 108 109 110 111) A (113) _ _ R T _ _ E . (115 116 117 118 119 120 121 122)

*See Solution on p. 184*

# Double Puzzle #3c

**A list of words that describe the Types of Commodities in the Stock Market**

FAINAICNL CIITMEOODMS
12 29 56 15 16 65 44 55 20 | 24 26 25 28 52 54

ERGENY
45 39 42 17 50

ELMTA
43 3

AUURGLTRICE
64 57 31 23 7 8 68 41

LCTSIOEVK NDA AMTE
60 18 5 21 14 | 6 38 | 32 30

FTOS CEDTMIIOOMS
69 11 | 58 35 46 36

PEOIRUCS SOETNS
9 | 1 67 53 61

FRESOT PCTORDUS
63 33 66 | 27 47 40

1 H(2) 3 | 5 6 7 8 9 | 11 12 | 14 15 16 17 18 B(19) 20 21 | 23 24 25 26 27 28 29 30 31 32 33

35 36 | 38 39 40 41 42 43 44 45 46 47 | B(49) 50 | 52 53 54 55 56 57 58 B(59) 60 61

63 64 65 66 67 68 69 .(70)

*See Solution on p. 184*

# Double Puzzle #3d

**A list of words that describe the Types of Stocks in the Stock Market**

PERRFEERD SCKOTS
49 4 45 51 64 61 75 81

CMMOON SOCKTS
16 67 12 22 15

BC-IEHULP SCTKOS
24 39 25 77 53 11 33 17 38

GOTRWH SOKTCS
9 73 74 14

EUAVL SOCKTS
31 76 65 18

DVEDNIID SOCKTS
7 3 1 42 8 6 66 41

DFEISEVNE SKTOCS
82 2 69 21 5 54

NYPEN SKTOCS
55 68 35 28 26 19 44 79

1 2 3 4 5 6 7 8 9   11 12   14 15 16 17 18 19   21 22   24 25 26 27 28 29 (I = 27, G = 29)   31

33 34 35 36 (I = 34, Y = 36)   38 39 40 41 42 (I = 40)   44 45   47 (A)   49 50 51 (I = 50)   53 54 55 56 57 58 (I = 56, N = 57, G = 58)   60 61 (I = 60)

63 64 65 66 67 68 69 (B = 63)   71 (A)   73 74 75 76 77   79 80 81 82 83 (A = 80, . = 83)

See Solution on p. 184

## Cryptogram #3a - The Trading Instruments in the Stock Market

| A | B | C | D | E | F | G | H | I | J | K | L | M | N | O | P | Q | R | S | T | U | V | W | X | Y | Z |
|---|---|---|---|---|---|---|---|---|---|---|---|---|---|---|---|---|---|---|---|---|---|---|---|---|---|
|   |   |   |   |   |   |   |   |   |   |   |   |   |   |   |   |   |   |   |   |   |   |   |   |   |   |

T K U Z N F B    N F E T K Y X L F T E    E Y G R    U E

E T I G W E    U F Z    H I F Z E    G U F    H L

U    J U P Y U H P L    C U M    T I

Z N J L K E N D M    U F    N F J L E T X L F T

V I K T D I P N I    U F Z    V I T L F T N U P P M

L U K F    U    D N F U F G N U P    K L T Y K F

*See Solution on p. 185*

## Cryptogram #3b - Type of Securities in the Stock Market

| A | B | C | D | E | F | G | H | I | J | K | L | M | N | O | P | Q | R | S | T | U | V | W | X | Y | Z |
|---|---|---|---|---|---|---|---|---|---|---|---|---|---|---|---|---|---|---|---|---|---|---|---|---|---|
| | | | | | | | | | | | | | | | | | | | | | | | | | |

R O Q G Y U R O A    R O    Y G M J X R U R G Y M S O

B X K Q R Z G    R O Z R Q R Z J S N Y    S O Z

P J Y R O G Y Y G Y    D R U I    U I G

K B B K X U J O R U E    U K    B K U G O U R S N N E

A X K D    U I G R X    D G S N U I    K Q G X

U R V G

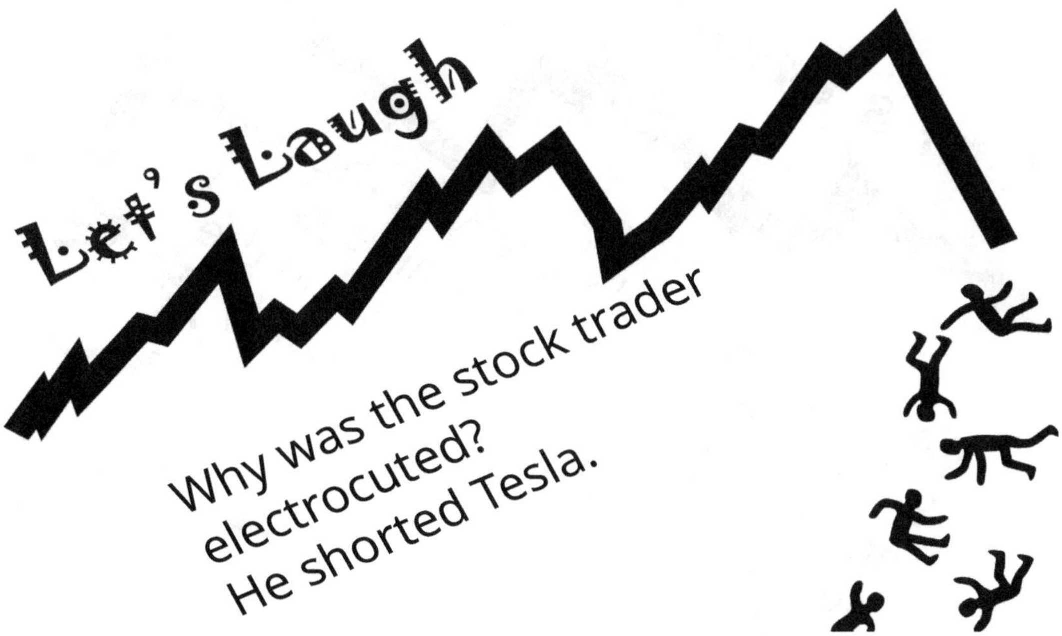


*See Solution on p. 185*

## Cryptogram #3c - Type of Commodities in the Stock Market

| A | B | C | D | E | F | G | H | I | J | K | L | M | N | O | P | Q | R | S | T | U | V | W | X | Y | Z |
|---|---|---|---|---|---|---|---|---|---|---|---|---|---|---|---|---|---|---|---|---|---|---|---|---|---|
| | | | | | | | | | | | | | | | | | | | | | | | | | |

N X L Q    D F M Q N V X Y N    T N Q

S X L L X B D V D Q N    N T S C    E N    R X I B

E F B    N D I M Q Y    E N    E    C Q B R Q

E R E D F N V    D F K I E V D X F    E F B

Q S X F X L D S    T F S Q Y V E D F V G

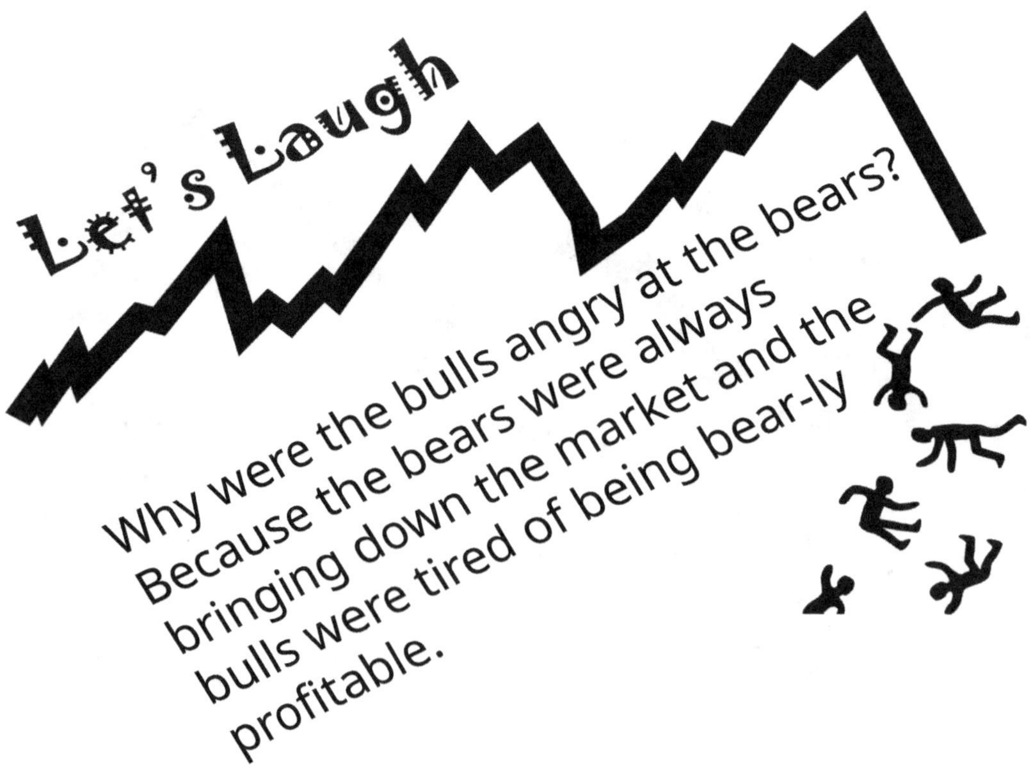


*See Solution on p. 185*

## Cryptogram #3d - Type of Stocks in the Stock Market

| A | B | C | D | E | F | G | H | I | J | K | L | M | N | O | P | Q | R | S | T | U | V | W | X | Y | Z |
|---|---|---|---|---|---|---|---|---|---|---|---|---|---|---|---|---|---|---|---|---|---|---|---|---|---|
|  |  |  |  |  |  |  |  |  |  |  |  |  |  |  |  |  |  |  |  |  |  |  |  |  |  |

REUI RKEOFR RDOT JR KTERI

EP QBDIOTVL OEULJZVIR JSI

FZEMZ PES KTIVS RKJQVBVKN

JZW RKIJWN SIKDSZR MTVBI

EKTISR RDOT JR KTERI EP

TVXTSVRF RKJSKDLR OJZ QI

UESI CEBJKVBI

See Solution on p. 185

# Related Words Matching #3a

## Associate Trading Instruments to their Related Words:

| | | | |
|---|---|---|---|
| 1 | CFDs | A | physical goods, agriculture, mining, energy, precious metals, industrial metals |
| 2 | Commodities | B | expiration, strike, premium, call, put, leverage |
| 3 | Currencies | C | index, diversification, asset allocation, passive investing, fund manager |
| 4 | Bonds | D | contract length, leverage, margin, spread, trade execution |
| 5 | Futures | E | trading, investing, portfolio, market, dividend |
| 6 | ETFs | F | exchange rate, forex trading, currency pair, spot market, forward market |
| 7 | Options | G | margin, settlement, delivery, long, short |
| 8 | Stocks | H | exchange rate, forex trading, currency pair, spot market, forward market |

*See Solution on p. 186*

# Related Words Matching #3b

## Associate Security Types to their Related Words:

| | | | |
|---|---|---|---|
| 1 | Options | A | investment, diversification, portfolio, fund manager, expense ratio |
| 2 | Futures | B | exchange-traded funds, index funds, passive investment, tracking error, asset allocation |
| 3 | Mutual funds | C | debt, fixed income, convertibility, conversion price, conversion ratio |
| 4 | ETFs | D | debt, fixed income, corporate bonds, government bonds, municipal bonds |
| 5 | Warrants | E | shares, equities, securities, common stock, preferred stock |
| 6 | Convertible bonds | F | warrants, derivatives, call options, put options, strike price |
| 7 | Stocks | G | contracts, derivatives, commodities, index futures, futures market |
| 8 | Bonds | H | options, derivatives, call warrants, put warrants, expiration date |

*See Solution on p. 186*

# Related Words Matching #3c

### Associate Commodity Types to their Related Words:

| | | | |
|---|---|---|---|
| 1 | Financial commodities | A | diamonds, emeralds, rubies, sapphires, pearls |
| 2 | Agriculture | B | cattle, pigs, poultry, lamb, beef |
| 3 | Energy | C | coffee, cocoa, sugar, cotton, wheat |
| 4 | Metal | D | currencies, interest rates, indexes, futures, options |
| 5 | Livestock and meat | E | lumber, paper, timber, pulp, wood |
| 6 | Soft commodities | F | oil, gas, electricity, renewable energy, fossil fuels |
| 7 | Forest products | G | iron, steel, aluminum, copper, gold |
| 8 | Precious stones | H | farming, crops, livestock, food, agribusiness |

*See Solution on p. 186*

# Related Words Matching #3d

## Associate Stock Types to their Related Words:

| | | | |
|---|---|---|---|
| 1 | Common stocks | A | large companies, stability, reputation, dividends, market leaders |
| 2 | Preferred stocks | B | small companies, high risk, low price, speculation, volatility |
| 3 | Blue-chip stocks | C | companies with steady, reliable performance, low volatility, stability, income, market downturns |
| 4 | Penny stocks | D | companies that pay regular dividends, income, yield, payout ratio, dividend yield |
| 5 | Growth stocks | E | shares, equities, securities, stock market, ownership |
| 6 | Value stocks | F | companies with low prices relative to their earnings, dividends, or assets, value investing, fundamental analysis, risk, return |
| 7 | Dividend stocks | G | shares, equities, securities, dividends, fixed income |
| 8 | Defensive stocks | H | companies with high potential for growth, earnings, price appreciation, risk, market trend |

*See Solution on p. 186*

### Trading Instruments in the Stock Market

- **John**: Hey Lucy, I don't understand some financial terms, can you explain them to me?
- **Lucy**: Sure, let's start with stocks, they're shares of ownership in a company.
- **John**: And options?
- **Lucy**: Options give the holder the right to buy or sell a specific stock at a specific price on or before a specific date.
- **John**: And futures?
- **Lucy**: Futures are contracts obligating the buyer to purchase a specific asset like a commodity or currency at a specific price in the future.
- **John**: And ETFs?
- **Lucy**: ETFs are collections of assets traded on stock exchanges, like a stock.
- **John**: And currencies and commodities?
- **Lucy**: Currencies are types of money like the US dollar or Euro, and commodities are natural resources like oil, gold, or wheat.
- **John**: What about bonds and CFDs?
- **Lucy**: Bonds are debt issued by companies or governments, CFDs are financial derivatives that allow speculation on price movements of underlying assets.
- **John**: Thank you, Lucy, that was really helpful.

## Multiple-Choice Quiz #3a: Circle the Correct Answer

1. **What is a stock?**
a) A collection of assets traded on stock exchanges
b) A form of debt issued by a company
c) A contract obligating the buyer to purchase a specific asset
d) A share of ownership in a company

2. **What does an option give the holder the right to do?**
a) Hedge against losses or speculate on future prices
b) Buy or sell a specific stock at a specific price on or before a specific date
c) Lend money to a company or government
d) Gain exposure to a specific market

3. **What is the purpose of a future contract?**
a) Obligate the buyer to purchase a specific asset
b) Give the holder the right to buy or sell a specific stock
c) Diversify a portfolio or gain exposure to a specific market
d) Allow speculation on price movements of underlying assets

4. **What is an ETF?**
a) A share of ownership in a company
b) A form of debt issued by a company
c) A contract obligating the buyer to purchase a specific asset
d) A collection of assets traded on stock exchanges

**Trading Instruments in the Stock Market**

- **John**: Hey Lucy, I don't understand some financial terms, can you explain them to me?
- **Lucy**: Sure, let's start with stocks, they're shares of ownership in a company.
- **John**: And options?
- **Lucy**: Options give the holder the right to buy or sell a specific stock at a specific price on or before a specific date.
- **John**: And futures?
- **Lucy**: Futures are contracts obligating the buyer to purchase a specific asset like a commodity or currency at a specific price in the future.
- **John**: And ETFs?
- **Lucy**: ETFs are collections of assets traded on stock exchanges, like a stock.
- **John**: And currencies and commodities?
- **Lucy**: Currencies are types of money like the US dollar or Euro, and commodities are natural resources like oil, gold, or wheat.
- **John**: What about bonds and CFDs?
- **Lucy**: Bonds are debt issued by companies or governments, CFDs are financial derivatives that allow speculation on price movements of underlying assets.
- **John**: Thank you, Lucy, that was really helpful.

# Multiple-Choice Quiz #3a: Circle the Correct Answer

| | |
|---|---|
| 5. **What are currencies?**<br>a) Natural resources like oil, gold, or wheat<br>b) Types of money like the US dollar or Euro<br>c) A form of debt issued by a company or government<br>d) A collection of assets traded on stock exchanges | 6. **What are commodities?**<br>a) Types of money like the US dollar or Euro<br>b) Natural resources like oil, gold, or wheat<br>c) A form of debt issued by a company or government<br>d) A collection of assets traded on stock exchanges |
| 7. **What is the purpose of bonds?**<br>a) A form of debt issued by a company or government<br>b) A contract obligating the buyer to purchase a specific asset<br>c) Give the holder the right to buy or sell a specific stock<br>d) Allow speculation on price movements of underlying assets | 8. **What is the main feature of CFDs?**<br>a) A form of debt issued by a company or government<br>b) Diversify a portfolio or gain exposure to a specific market<br>c) Allow speculation on price movements of underlying assets<br>d) Obligate the buyer to purchase a specific asset |
| 9. **What are examples of underlying assets that can be speculated on using CFDs?**<br>a) Stocks, currencies, commodities, or index b) Natural resources like oil, gold, or wheat<br>c) Types of money like the US dollar or Euro<br>d) A form of debt issued by a company or government | 10. **What is a stock option?**<br>a) A share of ownership in a company<br>b) The right to buy or sell a stock at a set price within a certain timeframe<br>c) A form of debt issued by a company or government<br>d) A natural resource like oil or gold |

*See Solution on p. 187*

**Types of Securities in the Stock Market**

**John**: Hey Lucy, can you help me with these terms? I've been hearing them around the office, but I don't know what they mean.
**Lucy**: Sure, let's start with stocks. They represent ownership in a company. When you buy a stock, you're buying a small piece of that company.
**John**: OK, got it. What about bonds?
**Lucy**: Bonds are loans that companies or governments make to investors. When you buy a bond, you're lending money to the issuer in exchange for interest payments.
**John**: And options?
**Lucy**: Options are contracts that give the right, but not the obligation, to buy or sell an asset at a specific price and time. They can be used for hedging or speculation.
**John**: Futures?
**Lucy**: Futures are similar, but the buyer is obligated to complete the transaction. They're commonly used for commodities and financial products.
**John**: Mutual funds and ETFs?
**Lucy**: Mutual funds are investment vehicles that pools money from different investors to buy a diversified portfolio. ETFs are similar, but trade like individual stocks.
**John**: Warrants and Convertible bonds?
**Lucy**: Warrants give the right, but not the obligation, to buy a company's stock at a specific price and time. Convertible bonds can be converted into shares at a specific price and time.
**John**: Got it, thanks for the help.
**Lucy**: My pleasure, let me know if you need more help.

# Multiple-Choice Quiz #3b: Circle the Correct Answer

| 1. **What type of security represents ownership in a company?**<br>a) Bonds<br>b) Options<br>c) Stocks<br>d) Futures | 2. **What type of security is a loan that companies or governments make to investors?**<br>a) Bonds<br>b) Options<br>c) Stocks<br>d) Futures |
|---|---|
| 3. **What type of contract gives investors the right, but not the obligation, to buy or sell a specific asset at a specific price on a specific date?**<br>a) Bonds<br>b) Options<br>c) Stocks<br>d) Futures | 4. **What type of contract obligates the buyer to complete the transaction?**<br>a) Bonds<br>b) Options<br>c) Futures<br>d) Mutual Funds |

**Types of Securities in the Stock Market**

**John**: Hey Lucy, can you help me with these terms? I've been hearing them around the office, but I don't know what they mean.
**Lucy**: Sure, let's start with stocks. They represent ownership in a company. When you buy a stock, you're buying a small piece of that company.
**John**: OK, got it. What about bonds?
**Lucy**: Bonds are loans that companies or governments make to investors. When you buy a bond, you're lending money to the issuer in exchange for interest payments.
**John**: And options?
**Lucy**: Options are contracts that give the right, but not the obligation, to buy or sell an asset at a specific price and time. They can be used for hedging or speculation.
**John**: Futures?
**Lucy**: Futures are similar, but the buyer is obligated to complete the transaction. They're commonly used for commodities and financial products.
**John**: Mutual funds and ETFs?
**Lucy**: Mutual funds are investment vehicles that pools money from different investors to buy a diversified portfolio. ETFs are similar, but trade like individual stocks.
**John**: Warrants and Convertible bonds?
**Lucy**: Warrants give the right, but not the obligation, to buy a company's stock at a specific price and time. Convertible bonds can be converted into shares at a specific price and time.
**John**: Got it, thanks for the help.
**Lucy**: My pleasure, let me know if you need more help.

# Multiple-Choice Quiz #3b: Circle the Correct Answer

5.**investment vehicle that pools money from investors to buy a portfolio of stocks, bonds, or other securities?**
a) ETFs
b) Options
c) Futures
d) Mutual Funds

6. **What type of investment vehicle is similar to mutual funds, but is traded on stock exchanges, like individual stocks?**
a) ETFs
b) Options
c) Futures
d) Bonds

7. **Type of security that gives investors the right, not the obligation, to buy a stock at a specific price and time?**
a) Warrants
b) Options
c) Futures
d) Mutual Funds

8. **What type of bond can be converted into shares of a company's stock at a specific price and at a specific time?**
a) Warrants
b) Options
c) Convertible Bonds
d) Mutual Funds

9. **When you buy a stock, you are essentially buying a small piece of that company.**
a) True
b) False

10. **When you buy a bond, you're lending money to the issuer in exchange for interest payments.**
a) True
b) False

*See Solution on p. 187*

### Types of Commodities in the Stock Market

- **John**: Hey Lucy, do you know what types of commodities are traded on the stock market?
- **Lucy**: Not really, but I heard that there are different types. Can you explain?

**John**: Sure, there are many types of commodities, but some of the most common include agriculture, energy, metal, livestock and meat, and soft commodities.

- **Lucy**: That sounds interesting, can you give me an example of agriculture commodities?
- **John**: Agriculture commodities include things like grains, such as wheat and corn, as well as things like coffee and cocoa.
- **Lucy**: Oh, I see. And what about energy commodities?
- **John**: Energy commodities include things like oil, natural gas, and electricity.
- **Lucy**: Interesting, and what about metal commodities?
- **John**: Metal commodities include things like gold, silver, and copper.
- **Lucy**: What about livestock and meat?
- **John**: Livestock and meat commodities include cattle, pigs, and poultry.
- **Lucy**: And what are soft commodities?
- **John**: Soft commodities include things like cotton, sugar, and rubber.
- **John**: oh and also forest products, Precious stones and Financial commodities are also traded in the market.
- **Lucy**: wow, there are so many types of commodities. Thanks for explaining it to me, John. Now I understand it better.

# Multiple-Choice Quiz #3c: Circle the Correct Answer

| | |
|---|---|
| 1. **What are some common types of commodities traded on the stock market?**<br>a) Agriculture, Energy, Metal, Livestock and Meat, Soft commodities<br>b) Technology, Automobiles, Real estate, Banking<br>c) Furniture, Books, Clothing, Food<br>d) Art, Music, Theater, Dance | 2. **Can you provide an example of an agriculture commodity?**<br>a) Wheat<br>b) Oil<br>c) Gold<br>d) Cattle |
| 3. **Can you provide an example of an energy commodity?**<br>a) Oil<br>b) Wheat<br>c) Gold<br>d) Cattle | 4. **Can you provide an example of a metal commodity?**<br>a) Gold<br>b) Oil<br>c) Wheat<br>d) Cattle |

**Types of Commodities in the Stock Market**

- **John**: Hey Lucy, do you know what types of commodities are traded on the stock market?
- **Lucy**: Not really, but I heard that there are different types. Can you explain?

**John**: Sure, there are many types of commodities, but some of the most common include agriculture, energy, metal, livestock and meat, and soft commodities.

- **Lucy**: That sounds interesting, can you give me an example of agriculture commodities?
- **John**: Agriculture commodities include things like grains, such as wheat and corn, as well as things like coffee and cocoa.
- **Lucy**: Oh, I see. And what about energy commodities?
- **John**: Energy commodities include things like oil, natural gas, and electricity.
- **Lucy**: Interesting, and what about metal commodities?
- **John**: Metal commodities include things like gold, silver, and copper.
- **Lucy**: What about livestock and meat?
- **John**: Livestock and meat commodities include cattle, pigs, and poultry.
- **Lucy**: And what are soft commodities?
- **John**: Soft commodities include things like cotton, sugar, and rubber.
- **John**: oh and also forest products, Precious stones and Financial commodities are also traded in the market.
- **Lucy**: wow, there are so many types of commodities. Thanks for explaining it to me, John. Now I understand it better.

## Multiple-Choice Quiz #3c: Circle the Correct Answer

| | |
|---|---|
| 5. **Can you provide an example of a livestock and meat commodity?**<br>a) Cattle<br>b) Oil<br>c) Gold<br>d) Wheat | 6. **Can you provide an example of a soft commodity?**<br>a) Cotton<br>b) Oil<br>c) Gold<br>d) Cattle |
| 7. **Has John mentioned other types of commodities traded in the market?**<br>a) Yes, forest products, Precious stones and Financial commodities<br>b) No, only the five mentioned are traded<br>c) Some other types are traded but not specified<br>d) There is no information available | 8. **What is an example of a forest product that is traded in the market?**<br>a) Timber<br>b) Gold<br>c) Oil<br>d) Cattle |
| 9. **What is an example of precious stone that is traded in the market?**<br>a) Diamond<br>b) Cotton<br>c) Gold<br>d) Poultry | 10. **What are the financial commodities that are traded in the market?**<br>a) Stock, Bonds, Options, Futures<br>b) Wheat, Corn, Coffee, Cocoa<br>c) Timber, Natural gas, electricity<br>d) Art, Music, Theater, Dance |

*See Solution on p. 187*

## Types of Stocks in the Stocks Market

**John**: Hey Lucy, have you heard about the different types of stocks?
**Lucy**: Not really, John. I feel intimidated by financial language. Can you help me?
**John**: Of course. Common stocks represent ownership in a company.
**Lucy**: Okay, got it. And what about preferred stocks?
**John**: Preferred stocks are similar to common stocks, but they have a higher claim on a company's assets and earnings. They usually pay a fixed dividend.
**Lucy**: And what are blue-chip stocks?
**John**: Blue-chip stocks are stocks of well-established and financially stable companies. They are considered less risky investments.
**Lucy**: And penny stocks?
**John**: Penny stocks are stocks that trade for less than $5 per share. They're considered more risky investments.
**Lucy**: And growth stocks?
John: Growth stocks are expected to grow faster than the market, but may not pay dividends.
**Lucy**: And value stocks?
**John**: Value stocks are considered undervalued by the market. They often pay dividends and have steady earnings growth.
**Lucy**: And dividend stocks?
**John**: Dividend stocks pay regular dividends to shareholders.
**Lucy**: And defensive stocks?
**John**: Defensive stocks are stocks of companies that are less affected by the economic cycle. They tend to pay high dividends.
**Lucy**: Thanks, John. Now I have a better understanding of all of these stock types.

# Multiple-Choice Quiz #3d: Circle the Correct Answer

| | |
|---|---|
| 1. **What type of stocks represent ownership in a company?**<br>a) Common stocks<br>b) Preferred stocks<br>c) Blue-chip stocks<br>d) Penny stocks | 2. **What type of stocks have a higher claim on a company's assets and earnings?**<br>a) Common stocks<br>b) Preferred stocks<br>c) Blue-chip stocks<br>d) Penny stocks |
| 3. **What type of stocks are of well-established and financially stable companies?**<br>a) Common stocks<br>b) Preferred stocks<br>c) Blue-chip stocks<br>d) Penny stocks | 4. **What type of stocks trade for less than $5 per share?**<br>a) Common stocks<br>b) Preferred stocks<br>c) Blue-chip stocks<br>d) Penny stocks |

**Types of Stocks in the Stocks Market**

**John**: Hey Lucy, have you heard about the different types of stocks?
**Lucy**: Not really, John. I feel intimidated by financial language. Can you help me?
**John**: Of course. Common stocks represent ownership in a company.
**Lucy**: Okay, got it. And what about preferred stocks?
**John**: Preferred stocks are similar to common stocks, but they have a higher claim on a company's assets and earnings. They usually pay a fixed dividend.
**Lucy**: And what are blue-chip stocks?
**John**: Blue-chip stocks are stocks of well-established and financially stable companies. They are considered less risky investments.
**Lucy**: And penny stocks?
**John**: Penny stocks are stocks that trade for less than $5 per share. They're more risky.
**Lucy**: And growth stocks?
John: Growth stocks are expected to grow faster than the market, but may not pay dividends.
**Lucy**: And value stocks?
**John**: Value stocks are considered undervalued by the market. They often pay dividends and have steady earnings growth.
**Lucy**: And dividend stocks?
**John**: Dividend stocks pay regular dividends to shareholders.
**Lucy**: And defensive stocks?
**John**: Defensive stocks are stocks of companies that are less affected by the economic cycle. They tend to pay high dividends.
**Lucy**: Thanks, John. Now I have a better understanding of all of these stock types.

# Multiple-Choice Quiz #3d: Circle the Correct Answer

| | |
|---|---|
| 5. **What type of stocks are expected to grow faster than the overall market?**<br>a) Common stocks<br>b) Growth stocks<br>c) Value stocks<br>d) Dividend stocks | 6. **What type of stocks are considered undervalued by the market?**<br>a) Common stocks<br>b) Growth stocks<br>c) Value stocks<br>d) Dividend stocks |
| 7. **What type of stocks pay regular dividends to shareholders?**<br>a) Common stocks<br>b) Growth stocks<br>c) Value stocks<br>d) Dividend stocks | 8. **Stocks less affected by the economic cycle and that tend to pay high dividends.**<br>a) Common stocks<br>b) Growth stocks<br>c) Value stocks<br>d) Defensive stocks |
| 9. **Stocks that pay a fixed dividend.**<br>a) Common stocks<br>b) Preferred stocks<br>c) Blue-chip stocks<br>d) Penny stocks | 10. **Has a higher claim on a company's assets and earnings, and pay a dividend.**<br>a) Common stocks<br>b) Growth stocks<br>c) Value stocks<br>d) Preferred stocks |

*See Solution on p. 187*

# Unit 4: Trading Types

In Unit 4, we will explore ten distinct trading types. It's important to understand the different types of trading because each type of trading involves its own set of risks and rewards and requires a different set of skills and strategies. Understanding the characteristics and strategies of each type of trading can help traders make more informed decisions about which type of trading is most suitable for their goals and risk tolerance.

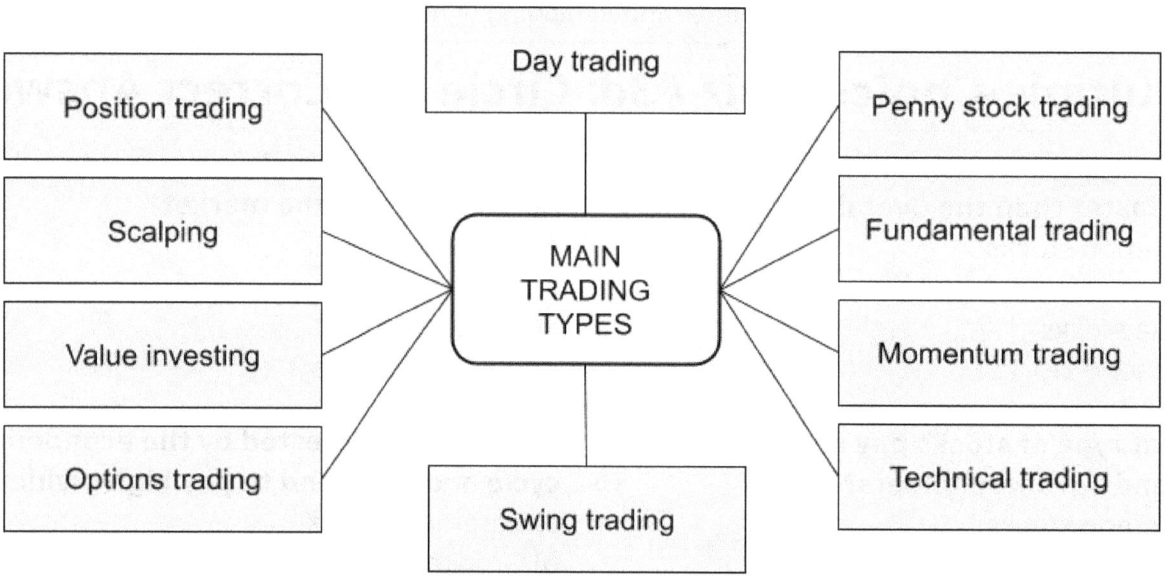


Overall, understanding these different types of trading can help traders make more informed decisions about which type of trading is most suitable for their goals and risk tolerance, and to use appropriate strategies and risk management techniques for that type of trading.

# Main Trading Types: Definitions

1. **Day trading**: Day trading is a high-pressure, high-stress type of trading that requires traders to be constantly monitoring the markets and making quick decisions. It can be a good option for traders who have a high risk tolerance and are comfortable with short-term volatility.

2. **Swing trading**: Swing trading is a more moderate-term strategy that typically involves holding positions for a period of several days to several weeks. It can be a good option for traders who have a moderate risk tolerance and are comfortable with moderate-term volatility.

3. **Position trading**: Position trading is a longer-term strategy that involves holding positions for a period of several weeks to several months, or even longer. It can be a good option for traders who have a lower risk tolerance and are comfortable with long-term volatility.

4. **Scalping**: Scalping is a high-frequency trading strategy that requires traders to make quick decisions and be able to execute trades quickly and efficiently. It can be a good option for traders who have a high risk tolerance and are comfortable with short-term volatility.

5. **Value investing**: This type of investing is a strategy where investors try to identify undervalued stocks and buy them at a price that is below their intrinsic value.

# Main Trading Types: Definitions

6. **Options Trading**: is a contract where the buyer has the right but not the obligation to buy or sell an underlying asset at a specific price and date. This type of trading requires more complex strategies and a good understanding of the underlying assets and derivatives market

7. **Penny stock trading**: this type of trading involves buying shares in smaller, less established companies that trade for less than $5 per share. It can be more risky than other types of trading, as these stocks are often more volatile and subject to greater market fluctuations

8. **Fundamental trading**: This type of trading refers to traders who focus on the underlying financial health of a company and make investment decisions based on financial metrics such as revenue, earnings, and cash flow.

9. **Momentum trading**: This type of trading focuses on the assets which are currently performing well and traders may invest in those assets which showing an upward trend

10. **Technical trading**: Technical traders use charts and technical indicators to analyze historical price and volume data to identify patterns and predict future price movements.

# Traders vs. Long-Term Investors

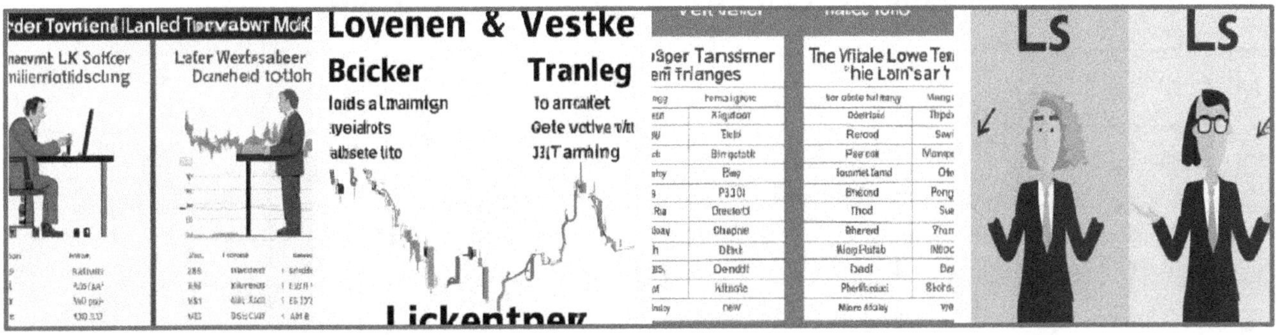


### What is the difference between a long-term investor and a trader?

A long-term investor is someone who holds securities for an extended period of time, typically several years or more. Long-term investors are generally more focused on the underlying fundamentals of the securities they hold and are less concerned with short-term price fluctuations. They are often seeking to build wealth over the long term by buying and holding securities that they believe will appreciate in value over time.

A trader, on the other hand, is someone who actively buys and sells securities with the goal of making a profit from price movements in the market. Traders may hold positions for a few minutes, a few days, or a few weeks, depending on the specific trading strategy they are using. They are generally more focused on short-term price movements and may use a variety of techniques, such as technical analysis or momentum trading, to make informed trading decisions.

In general, it could be said that the stock market has more long-term investors than traders, as long-term investment is generally seen as a way to build wealth over time while day trading or short-term investments tend to be more speculative and carry more risk.

Overall, the main difference between a long-term investor and a trader is the time frame in which they hold their securities. Long-term investors are focused on the long-term appreciation of their investments, while traders are focused on making profits from short-term price movements.

**Did You Know?**

Did you know? Studies have shown that many traders are more likely to suffer from overconfidence bias, which can lead to excessive trading, while long-term investors tend to be more patient and disciplined in their investment approach.

## Word Search Puzzle #4 - Different Types of Trading

Find the different trading types in the list below:

| | | | | | | | | | | | | | | | |
|---|---|---|---|---|---|---|---|---|---|---|---|---|---|---|---|
| M | M | S | V | M | Q | H | L | O | J | I | E | S | U | P | T |
| O | O | U | W | A | A | N | N | C | G | U | M | Q | V | O | E |
| M | V | P | S | I | D | S | X | U | H | U | R | E | A | S | C |
| E | D | A | T | C | N | F | Q | M | G | A | C | S | I | I | H |
| N | P | A | L | I | A | G | S | S | Y | C | A | M | A | T | N |
| T | Q | Y | Y | U | O | L | T | R | N | K | Y | Y | Q | I | I |
| U | X | H | B | T | E | N | P | R | W | M | R | U | I | O | C |
| M | B | X | J | L | R | I | S | I | A | K | E | Q | Y | N | A |
| T | E | H | O | E | W | A | N | T | N | D | I | Z | P | T | L |
| R | E | C | K | C | Q | A | D | V | R | G | I | H | A | R | T |
| A | Q | H | U | C | L | O | V | I | E | A | Q | N | B | A | R |
| D | N | D | J | K | T | B | J | L | N | S | D | K | G | D | A |
| I | Q | W | O | N | D | E | C | S | F | G | T | I | X | I | D |
| N | D | D | F | B | S | Q | K | A | S | B | R | I | N | N | I |
| G | R | A | R | V | X | Z | G | C | V | C | M | U | N | G | N |
| Q | Y | S | U | J | Q | U | O | C | K | F | B | P | B | G | G |

DAY TRADING
OPTIONS TRADING
SCALPING
TECHNICAL TRADING
MOMENTUM TRADING
POSITION TRADING
SWING TRADING
VALUE INVESTING

*See Solution on p. 188*

# Crossword Puzzle #4

## Learn about Trading Types

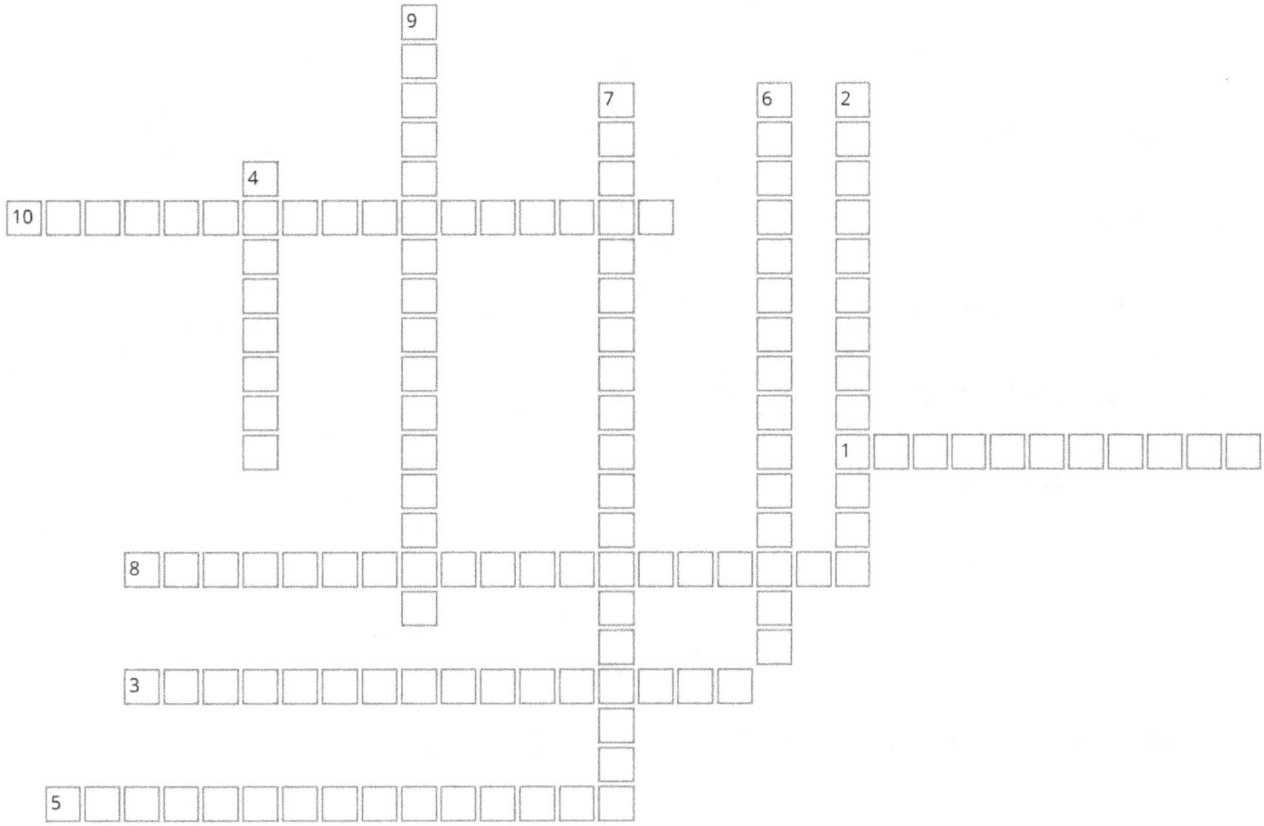


Across

**[1]** High-pressure, quick decision making trading strategy.

**[3]** Long-term strategy of holding positions for several weeks to months or longer.

**[5]** Strategy of identifying undervalued stocks and buying at a lower price.

**[8]** Investment strategy based on financial metrics such as revenue, earnings, and cash flow.

**[10]** Use of charts and indicators to identify patterns and predict price movements.

Down

**[2]** Moderate-term strategy of holding positions for several days to weeks.

**[4]** High-frequency trading strategy focused on quick trades and small profits.

**[6]** Contract allowing to buy or sell an underlying asset at a specific price and date.

**[7]** Buying shares of smaller, less established companies trading below $5 per share.

**[9]** Investment strategy that focus on currently performing assets.

*See Solution on p. 188*

## Scramble Puzzle #4 - Different Trading Types

**Uncramble the different trading types in the list below**

AYD TNIRDAG

TICEACNHL TNIRDAG

FAMNDUNEATL TADNRIG

PIISOOTN TDRINAG

MNTOMUEM TDINRAG

GNSIW TDIANRG

OOPNITS TNIARDG

ULVEA INTSINVEG

NYEPN COSKT TNRADIG

SICANPLG

*See Solution on p. 188*

# Definition Match-Up #4

## Trading Types

### Associate the *Trading Types* to their Definitions

| | | | |
|---|---|---|---|
| 1 | Momentum trading | A | High-frequency trading strategy focused on quick trades and small profits |
| 2 | Swing trading | B | Long-term strategy of holding positions for several weeks to months or longer |
| 3 | Day trading | C | Identifying undervalued stocks and buying at a lower price |
| 4 | Position trading | D | Investment strategy based on financial metrics such as revenue, earnings, and cash flow |
| 5 | Scalping | E | A moderate-term strategy of holding positions for several days to weeks |
| 6 | Options trading | F | High-pressure, quick decision-making trading strategy |
| 7 | Technical trading | G | Investment strategy that focuses on currently performing assets |
| 8 | Fundamental trading | H | Contract allowing to buy or sell an underlying asset at a specific price and date |
| 9 | Value investing | I | Buying shares of smaller, less established companies trading below $5 per share |
| 10 | Penny stock trading | J | Use of charts and indicators to identify patterns and predict price movements |

*See Solution on p. 188*

# Cloze Test #4

## Fill In the Blanks Using the 10 Trading Types below:

| Options trading - Penny stock trading - Scalping - Day trading - Fundamental trading - Momentum trading - Value investing - Technical trading - Position trading - Swing trading |
|---|

There are many different approaches to trading in the stock market, and each approach has its own set of advantages and disadvantages. a) __________ is when you buy and sell stocks within the same trading day, while b) __________ is when you hold onto a stock for a few days to a few weeks. c) __________ is when you hold onto a stock for a longer period of time, usually months to a year. d) __________ is a type of day trading where you try to make a small profit by buying and selling a stock multiple times within the same day. e) __________ is when you buy stocks that are gaining momentum, or increasing in price quickly. f) __________ is when you buy stocks that are undervalued by the market, with the hope that their value will increase in the future. g) __________, h) __________, i)__________, and j) __________ are also different ways of approaching the stock market, each with its own set of risks and rewards. Ultimately, the key is to understand your goals, risk tolerance, and the different strategies available to you, so you can make informed decisions and find the approach that works best for you.

**N.B.** The order of the answers from g) to j) is interchangeable.

*See Solution on p. 189*

# Missing Vowel #4

## Learn about Different Trading Types

| Puzzle | Clue |
| --- | --- |
| V _ L _ _   _ N V _ S T _ N G | Identifying undervalued stocks and buying at a lower price. |
| T _ C H N _ C _ L   T R _ D _ N G | Use of charts and indicators to identify patterns and predict price movements. |
| S W _ N G   T R _ D _ N G | Moderate-term strategy of holding positions for several days to weeks. |
| S C _ L P _ N G | High-frequency trading strategy focused on quick trades and small profits. |
| P _ S _ T _ _ N   T R _ D _ N G | Long-term strategy of holding positions for several weeks to months or longer. |
| P _ N N Y   S T _ C K   T R _ D _ N G | Buying shares of smaller, less established companies trading below $5 per share. |
| _ P T _ _ N S   T R _ D _ N G | Contract allowing to buy or sell an underlying asset at a specific price and date. |
| M _ M _ N T _ M   T R _ D _ N G | Investment strategy that focus on currently performing assets. |
| F _ N D _ M _ N T _ L   T R _ D _ N G | Investment strategy based on financial metrics such as revenue, earnings, and cash flow. |
| D _ Y   T R _ D _ N G | The buying and selling of securities within the same day. |

*See Solution on p. 189*

**Trading Types in the Stock Market**

- **George**: Hey Sandra, I've been thinking about trying my hand at trading on the stock market, but I don't know where to begin. Can you help me out?
- **Sandra**: Of course, George. What kind of trading are you interested in?
- **George**: Well, I've heard of day trading, swing trading, and position trading. Can you explain the differences between those?
- **Sandra**: Sure. Day trading is when you buy and sell stocks within the same trading day. Swing trading is when you hold onto a stock for a few days to a few weeks. Position trading is when you hold onto a stock for a longer period of time, usually months to a year.
- **George**: Hmm, I think I like the idea of position trading. What about scalping, momentum trading, and value investing?
- **Sandra**: Scalping is a type of day trading where you try to make a small profit by buying and selling a stock multiple times within the same day. Momentum trading is when you buy stocks that are gaining momentum, or increasing in price quickly. Value investing is when you buy stocks that are undervalued by the market, with the hope that their value will increase in the future.
- **George**: I see, thanks for explaining that. And what about options trading, penny stock trading, fundamental trading, and technical trading?

Sandra: You can research these other types of trading as you gain more knowledge and experience. Remember, always do your research and be aware of the risks before you start trading.

# Multiple-Choice Quiz #4: Circle the Correct Answer

1. **What is the main difference between day trading and position trading?**
a) The holding period of the stock
b) The type of stock traded
c) The amount of profit made

2. **In momentum trading, what is the main factor considered when buying stocks?**
a) The company's financials
b) The stock's price increase
c) The stock's dividends

3. **In value investing, what is the main goal?**
a) To buy undervalued stocks with the expectation that their value will increase
b) To make quick profits by buying and selling stocks multiple times within a day
c) To hold onto a stock for a few days to a few weeks

4. **How is scalping different from day trading?**
a) Scalping = making multiple daily trades for small profits, day trading = buying and selling stocks anytime during the day.
b) It is only applicable to penny stocks while day trading is applicable to all stocks
c) It is only for experienced traders while day trading is for all traders

5. **What are the risks of options trading?**
a) The risk of the underlying asset not reaching the strike price
b) The risk of the options expiring worthless
c) Both A and B

6. **Which one relies more on historical data and chart patterns?**
a) Fundamental trading
b) Technical trading
c) Both are equally dependent

### Trading Types in the Stock Market

- **George**: Hey Sandra, I've been thinking about trying my hand at trading on the stock market, but I don't know where to begin. Can you help me out?
- **Sandra**: Of course, George. What kind of trading are you interested in?
- **George**: Well, I've heard of day trading, swing trading, and position trading. Can you explain the differences between those?
- **Sandra**: Sure. Day trading is when you buy and sell stocks within the same trading day. Swing trading is when you hold onto a stock for a few days to a few weeks. Position trading is when you hold onto a stock for a longer period of time, usually months to a year.
- **George**: Hmm, I think I like the idea of position trading. What about scalping, momentum trading, and value investing?
- **Sandra**: Scalping is a type of day trading where you try to make a small profit by buying and selling a stock multiple times within the same day. Momentum trading is when you buy stocks that are gaining momentum, or increasing in price quickly. Value investing is when you buy stocks that are undervalued by the market, with the hope that their value will increase in the future.
- **George**: I see, thanks for explaining that. And what about options trading, penny stock trading, fundamental trading, and technical trading?
- **Sandra:** You can research these other types of trading as you gain more knowledge and experience. Remember, always do your research and be aware of the risks before you start trading.

## Multiple-Choice Quiz #4: Circle the Correct Answer

| | |
|---|---|
| 7. **What is penny stock trading?**<br>a) Trading stocks that have a low market value and are traded for less than $5 per share<br>b) Trading options contracts<br>c) Trading foreign stocks | 8. **What is the advice that Sandra gives to George before he starts trading?**<br>a) To start trading immediately<br>b) To research and be aware of the risks<br>c) To not start trading at all |
| 9. **What is the main difference between Swing Trading and Day Trading?**<br>a) The holding period of the stock<br>b) The type of stock traded<br>c) The amount of profit made | 10. **What is the main focus of Fundamental Trading?**<br>a) Analyzing historical data and chart patterns<br>b) Evaluating a company's financials to determine the intrinsic value of its stock<br>c) Following market momentum |

*See Solution on p. 189*

# Double Puzzle #4

## A list of words that describe different Trading Types in the Stock Market

AYD TADINRG — 73 13 / 77 65

WINGS TDRINAG — 43 120 / 104 28

PSITOOIN TINRADG — 19 55 57 130 5 / 10 23 24 68 82 27

SALICNPG — 41 100 1 12 2 89 90

MMNTUOEM TANIRDG — 34 31 81 35 22 33 8 / 4

LVUEA ITENVISNG — 30 113 97 53 / 78 67 58 103 75

OINTPOS TADINRG — 76 66 45 121 109 / 44 86 9 7 38

YNPEN TKSOC TDINRAG — 3 11 71 / 114 37 83 47 / 54 94 123 106 26 99

FENAMUTDANL TNRIADG — 20 40 25 112 49 63 105 74 / 79 51 50 118

THICENACL TINRADG — 61 46 80 62 32 / 64 60

1 2 3 4 5 X(6) 7 8 9 10 11 12 13 · 7(15) 0(16) %(17) · 19 20 · 22 23 24 25 26 27 28

30 31 32 33 34 35 · 37 38 · 40 41 · 43 44 45 46 47 · 49 50 51 K(52) 53 54 55 · 57 58

60 61 62 63 64 65 66 67 68 · B(70) 71 · 73 74 75 76 77 78 79 80 81 82 83 · O(85) 86

H(88) 89 90 H(91) -(92) F(93) 94 E(95) Q(96) 97 E(98) 99 100 Y(101) · 103 104 105 106 E(107) R(108) 109 ,(110) · 112 113 114 O(115) · K(117) 118 O(119) 120 121

123 S(124) · R(126) O(127) B(128) O(129) 130 S(131) .(132)

See Solution on p. 190

## Cryptogram #4 - Trading Types in the Stock Market

| A | B | C | D | E | F | G | H | I | J | K | L | M | N | O | P | Q | R | S | T | U | V | W | X | Y | Z |
|---|---|---|---|---|---|---|---|---|---|---|---|---|---|---|---|---|---|---|---|---|---|---|---|---|---|
| | | | | | | | | | | | | | | | | | | | | | | | | | |

W E S I S   F I S   Q U D K W I B S Z   B K   W E S

L U I C M   W E F W   E F J S   K U   Z W U Q X

T F I X S W   F W   F C C   Z D Q E   F Z

K U I W E   X U I S F   Q D V F   F K M   Z O I B F

*See Solution on p. 190*

# Related Words Matching #4

**Associate Trading Instruments to their Related Words:**

| | | | |
|---|---|---|---|
| 1 | Position trading | A | Short-term, Intraday, Speculation, Volatility, Liquidity |
| 2 | Value investing | B | Long-term, Investing, Hold, Appreciation, Diversification |
| 3 | Fundamental trading | C | Quick, Profit, Margin, Speed, Volume |
| 4 | Options trading | D | Trend, Rotation, Breakout, Follow-through, Volatility |
| 5 | Technical trading | E | Value, Income, Dividend, Bargain, Undervalued |
| 6 | Momentum trading | F | Derivative, Leverage, Hedging, Speculation, Volatility |
| 7 | Scalping | G | Speculation, Risk, Volatility, Small cap, Illiquid |
| 8 | Swing trading | H | Analysis, Earnings, Balance sheet, Cash flow, Valuation |
| 9 | Penny stock trading | I | Chart, Indicator, Trend, Pattern, Support/Resistance |
| 10 | Day trading | J | Intermediate-term, Trend, Position, Timing, Analysis |

*See Solution on p. 190*

# Unit 5: Bull and Bear Markets

Have you ever wondered about the significance of the terms "bulls" and "bears" in the stock market? These terms "Bulls" and "Bears" refer to the two different kinds of investors in the stock market. Bulls are investors who are optimistic about the market and expect prices to rise, while Bears are investors who are pessimistic and expect stock prices to fall. Bulls tend to buy stocks and commodities in the expectation of a price increase, while bears sell stocks and commodities in anticipation of a decline in price.

That is the reason there are two distinct types of markets: "Bull markets" and "Bear markets." A bull market is a period of time during which stock prices are rising or are expected to rise. This is typically characterized by a high level of investor confidence and optimism, and it can be fueled by a variety of factors, such as strong economic growth, low unemployment, and favorable corporate earnings. In a bull market, investors may be more willing to take on risk and buy stocks, as they believe that prices will continue to rise and that they will be able to sell their stocks at a profit in the future. Conversely, a bear market is a period of time during which stock prices are falling or are expected to fall, and is characterized by a lack of investor confidence and pessimism.

Overall, understanding these different types of trading can help traders make more informed decisions about which type of trading is most suitable for their goals and risk tolerance, and to use appropriate strategies and risk management techniques for that type of trading.

# Unit 5: Bull and Bear Markets

## Is the Stock Market a Zero-Sum Game?

A zero-sum what? In a way, we can say that the stock market is a zero-sum game, that is, for every bull who makes money, there must be a bear who loses money. It's like a game where the total gains and losses always add up to zero. It's important to note, however, that this only applies to individual transactions, not to the market as a whole.

For example, if you and your friend are playing a game of chess, and you win, it means your friend loses. The total winnings and losses of the game always add up to zero. When some people make money, others lose money. In the end, the amount of money gained by some people equals the amount lost by others.

Also, it's worth mentioning that sometimes new shares of stock are created, and this can change the zero-sum game concept, meaning that the overall value of the market can increase, but at any given time, the gains of one person come at the expense of another. So, it's like a game, where the total gains and losses always add up to zero, but with some exceptions.

**Did You Know?**

Did you know that, in general, there are more bulls than bears in the stock market? A bull market with rising stock prices and optimism about future economic growth tends to attract more investors, while a bear market with falling stock prices and pessimism about future economic growth tends to deter them.

# Unit 5: Bull and Bear Markets

## Characteristics of Bull Markets

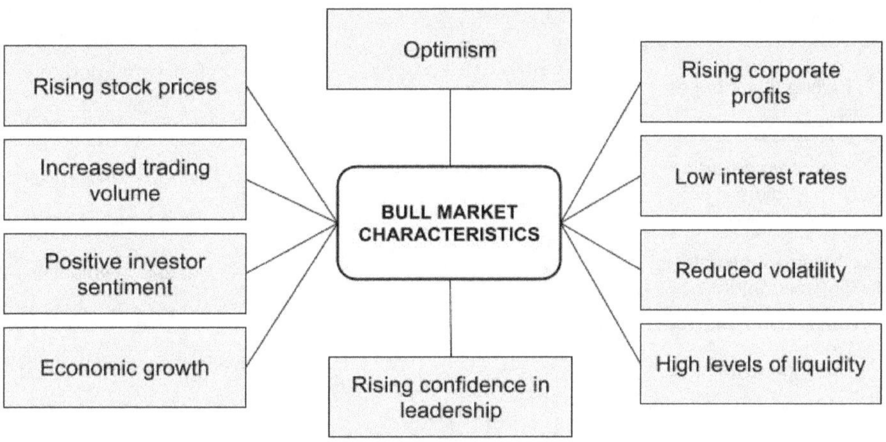


### Bull Market

- **Stock prices going up**: Prices are increasing over a period of time.
- **More trading**: More people are buying and selling shares.
- **Positive attitude**: Investors are hopeful about the market.
- **Economic growth**: The economy is doing well and people have jobs.
- **Companies making more money**: Companies are making more money.
- **Low borrowing costs**: It is cheap to borrow money.
- **Fewer ups and downs**: The market is not changing as much.
- **Plenty of money to invest**: There is a lot of money to invest.
- **Leadership is trusted**: People trust the people in charge.
- **Optimism**: Investors are hopeful about the future.

# Unit 5: Bull and Bear Markets

## Characteristics of Bear Markets

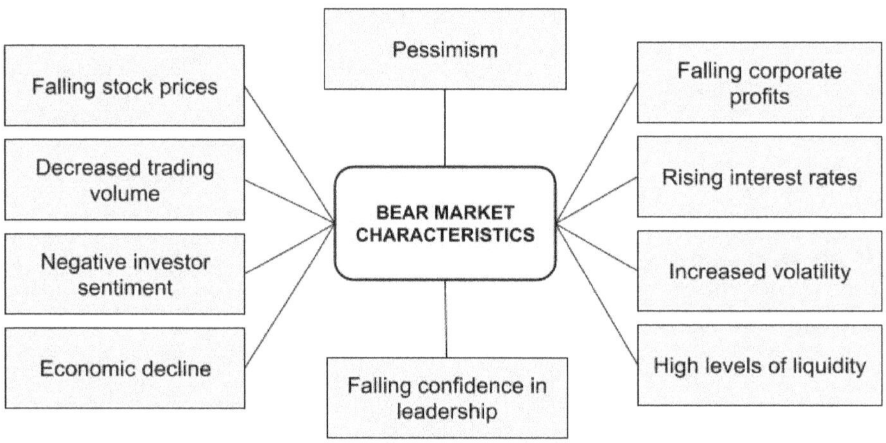


### Bear Market

- **Stock prices going down**: Prices are decreasing over a period of time.
- **Less trading**: Fewer people are buying and selling shares.
- **Negative attitude**: Investors are not hopeful about the market.
- **Economic decline**: The economy is not doing well, and many people don't have jobs.
- **Companies making less money**: Companies are making less money.
- **High borrowing costs**: It is expensive to borrow money.
- **More ups and downs**: The market is changing a lot.
- **Less money to invest**: There is not much money to invest.
- **Leadership is not trusted**: People don't trust the people in charge.
- **Pessimism**: Investors are not hopeful about the future.

# Word Search Puzzle #5a - Bull and Bear Markets

**Find Different Characteristics of Bull Markets in the list below:**

| P | B | S | S | T | I | F | O | R | P | E | T | A | R | O | P | R | O | C | G | N | I | S | I | R | D | U | E | W |
|---|---|---|---|---|---|---|---|---|---|---|---|---|---|---|---|---|---|---|---|---|---|---|---|---|---|---|---|---|
| J | O | B | E | K | M | H | X | C | O | V | P | C | Z | K | I | N | R | P | B | E | O | D | Y | D | P | T | I | B |
| A | F | S | D | O | B | G | Q | P | X | K | R | P | Z | O | O | M | S | W | Y | S | H | J | C | Y | M | S | Q | U |
| D | Y | F | I | H | V | I | N | C | R | E | A | S | E | D | T | R | A | D | I | N | G | V | O | L | U | M | E | A |
| O | J | T | H | T | U | N | G | F | U | R | Y | M | I | Q | O | P | E | P | A | K | Q | I | U | Q | O | T | D | I |
| M | B | Q | I | I | I | D | Z | K | T | A | E | G | G | V | U | A | U | J | R | J | L | F | E | C | N | X | D | R |
| U | W | R | R | L | G | V | V | C | G | F | E | C | Z | I | N | L | C | I | T | I | M | K | X | R | X | X | G | T |
| W | N | C | A | Z | I | H | E | Z | E | E | W | B | O | Q | Q | O | R | L | U | Y | A | Q | F | Y | K | Y | K | Z |
| U | G | L | F | D | O | T | L | I | D | N | U | W | Q | N | Q | A | P | B | H | C | R | V | D | R | Y | O | I | C |
| U | P | O | P | Q | S | N | A | E | N | T | L | R | I | N | O | H | M | Y | S | Y | F | O | C | A | E | W | I | G |
| U | V | W | C | U | Z | I | M | L | V | V | F | U | T | V | Z | M | J | C | Q | S | M | V | Q | F | M | V | G | Q |
| I | W | I | C | A | S | W | V | D | O | E | E | X | V | C | C | N | I | G | N | V | Z | Q | L | D | G | S | J | A |
| I | I | N | P | K | C | N | D | R | K | V | L | S | G | H | S | Z | W | C | S | N | C | K | H | K | K | E | I | N |
| H | S | T | Z | U | L | W | N | N | X | Q | D | S | T | J | P | Y | L | E | G | O | V | X | Z | A | A | C | O | Z |
| N | L | E | S | F | V | W | B | P | Q | A | C | E | O | O | S | X | K | W | P | R | N | F | H | A | Y | I | C | Z |
| R | A | R | R | T | G | V | M | E | K | J | F | U | C | F | R | C | L | N | A | I | O | C | D | D | A | R | G | B |
| L | Q | E | V | J | Y | Y | D | I | W | W | X | B | S | U | L | S | U | I | V | U | S | W | J | E | I | P | V | Z |
| R | S | S | F | R | O | P | T | I | M | I | S | M | D | A | D | I | E | V | S | L | A | Y | T | W | K | K | N | H |
| V | K | T | Z | S | H | O | M | Q | V | D | X | Z | J | C | X | E | Q | N | B | Y | J | D | E | H | Q | C | W | W |
| V | U | R | D | V | O | V | E | M | I | E | M | B | F | U | N | E | R | U | T | A | E | V | S | B | J | O | U | M |
| A | R | A | S | F | I | M | C | Y | J | K | D | N | Y | R | U | Y | S | D | I | I | E | U | O | T | D | T | M | O |
| T | C | T | U | L | P | S | W | Y | U | L | N | P | B | R | Y | D | T | C | Y | D | M | J | R | G | K | S | G | W |
| E | L | E | A | U | W | K | V | M | L | V | Q | G | A | R | R | D | O | F | P | O | I | E | W | B | L | G | D | Z |
| W | S | S | Y | T | B | U | C | D | R | W | W | Z | N | T | J | R | F | N | N | W | Y | T | N | Q | F | N | T | O |
| D | N | O | Y | E | U | X | X | W | H | Z | L | I | Q | C | A | F | J | I | Y | L | P | X | Y | T | P | I | W | O |
| C | R | L | G | Y | Q | G | W | M | D | X | V | I | I | G | J | D | L | A | O | R | E | X | P | J | Q | S | P | R |
| R | I | S | I | N | G | C | O | N | F | I | D | E | N | C | E | I | N | L | E | A | D | E | R | S | H | I | P | Y |
| Q | R | L | F | V | N | N | I | B | T | V | S | Q | K | Z | U | V | I | E | J | I | I | D | U | C | P | R | I | Z |
| B | F | T | L | Z | O | Z | N | J | D | T | W | V | J | O | S | Q | R | S | B | U | D | Y | V | A | Z | K | A | I |

ECONOMIC GROWTH
OPTIMISM
RISING CONFIDENCE IN LEADERSHIP
HIGH LEVELS OF LIQUIDITY
POSITIVE INVESTOR SENTIMENT
INCREASED TRADING VOLUME
REDUCED VOLATILITY
RISING CORPORATE PROFITS
LOW INTEREST RATES
RISING STOCK PRICES

*See Solution on p. 190*

# Word Search Puzzle #5b - Bull and Bear Markets

**Find the Different Characteristics of Bear Markets in the list below:**

| L | W | E | M | U | L | O | V | G | N | I | D | A | R | T | D | E | S | A | E | R | C | E | D | S | E | W | D | I |
|---|---|---|---|---|---|---|---|---|---|---|---|---|---|---|---|---|---|---|---|---|---|---|---|---|---|---|---|---|
| D | F | A | L | L | I | N | G | S | T | O | C | K | P | R | I | C | E | S | J | X | X | K | Z | J | L | U | I | W |
| H | I | O | T | E | C | O | N | O | M | I | C | D | E | C | L | I | N | E | Q | J | M | U | Q | N | G | Z | J | D |
| I | Y | V | G | N | P | S | V | I | G | R | I | I | N | E | Y | W | K | X | H | O | A | V | O | G | Z | O | M | R |
| M | U | J | R | P | F | L | T | H | Y | T | I | D | I | U | Q | I | L | F | O | S | L | E | V | E | L | W | O | L |
| Z | X | N | C | E | B | J | X | I | F | K | Y | C | M | X | B | Z | W | D | E | P | E | S | E | A | B | Y | H | E |
| G | P | X | P | L | F | F | C | A | F | S | E | Q | I | I | V | I | Y | A | V | K | U | G | V | R | G | K | Z | I |
| P | H | V | R | Y | N | M | Q | G | D | O | H | X | E | H | T | Z | R | H | P | R | Y | M | I | G | H | M | G | G |
| X | Q | X | C | N | B | U | F | N | K | P | R | S | A | R | V | S | J | G | T | T | J | S | H | L | A | H | B | K |
| C | K | D | B | G | Z | L | T | F | U | G | M | P | S | G | K | G | X | Q | I | O | I | X | K | Z | T | E | I | Y |
| U | M | B | W | L | F | D | F | N | Y | H | H | M | E | O | K | P | A | L | N | N | W | E | M | X | O | B | V | X |
| I | O | J | T | N | Y | F | V | G | B | M | S | Y | M | T | I | L | I | W | G | L | Z | C | J | P | A | J | A | G |
| W | Q | M | U | I | E | P | E | S | S | I | M | I | S | M | A | T | W | I | C | A | N | Z | S | S | B | C | Y | I |
| T | R | V | T | A | S | S | N | N | R | O | A | U | Q | F | A | R | N | X | W | U | A | T | Y | Z | P | Y | M | J |
| H | Q | Q | G | G | M | B | S | K | K | L | D | O | U | L | E | T | O | Q | Z | J | E | K | F | C | Y | M | V | K |
| Z | L | B | L | Z | B | L | H | U | U | P | O | W | O | G | E | Y | D | P | X | I | C | I | A | N | O | C | H | H |
| H | A | O | H | X | Q | T | Q | C | D | C | R | V | J | R | I | O | A | K | R | V | I | Q | B | B | E | Y | H | F |
| Q | O | Y | M | O | O | C | T | P | K | E | D | E | E | R | L | T | V | I | G | O | V | T | Z | F | E | D | L | T |
| X | P | K | D | M | R | T | B | T | J | E | V | S | T | M | B | Y | O | N | H | G | C | C | R | T | A | L | G | D |
| K | F | U | L | F | D | X | L | W | S | A | T | B | B | K | X | P | T | J | V | Y | D | G | S | X | V | X | A | O |
| L | J | W | Q | S | I | S | Y | A | X | R | C | C | O | D | L | P | N | U | Q | B | F | M | N | P | Z | C | V | S |
| A | Y | K | M | U | Q | R | E | H | A | J | K | I | F | W | H | A | O | C | W | D | K | I | Y | I | F | M | G | L |
| Y | X | C | I | N | U | R | T | T | R | O | X | C | H | D | H | H | I | W | R | K | H | H | N | X | L | B | E | Z |
| P | K | Z | X | P | C | Y | E | D | F | Q | W | G | Z | W | E | U | Z | H | Z | M | G | W | E | G | Y | L | H | Z |
| G | Q | F | M | N | I | S | W | N | O | W | G | B | W | W | X | P | M | B | F | B | N | D | Y | U | U | Q | A | F |
| G | R | D | I | E | Y | I | Q | Z | M | Y | H | F | W | R | W | A | Z | L | Y | T | O | S | V | Z | O | U | P | F |
| R | F | U | S | Z | U | P | C | U | H | Y | H | L | O | S | V | T | C | L | L | D | W | F | P | F | W | H | J | Y |
| N | E | G | A | T | I | V | E | I | N | V | E | S | T | O | R | S | E | N | T | I | M | E | N | T | J | N | M | S |
| F | A | L | L | I | N | G | C | O | N | F | I | D | E | N | C | E | I | N | L | E | A | D | E | R | S | H | I | P |

DECREASED TRADING VOLUME
FALLING CORPORATE PROFITS
NEGATIVE INVESTOR SENTIMENT
ECONOMIC DECLINE
FALLING STOCK PRICES
PESSIMISM
FALLING CONFIDENCE IN LEADERSHIP
INCREASED VOLATILITY
RISING INTEREST RATES
LOW LEVELS OF LIQUIDITY

*See Solution on p. 190*

# Crossword Puzzle #5a - Bull and Bear Markets

## Learn about the characteristics of Bull Markets in the list below:

Across

**[2]** People trust the people in charge.

**[4]** The market is not changing as much.

**[5]** It is cheap to borrow money.

**[9]** More people are buying and selling shares.

**[10]** Prices are increasing over a period of time.

Down

**[1]** Investors are hopeful about the future.

**[3]** There is a lot of money to invest.

**[6]** Companies are making more money.

**[7]** The economy is doing well and people have jobs.

**[8]** Investors are hopeful about the market.

*See Solution on p. 191*

# Crossword Puzzle #5b - Bull and Bear Markets

## Learn about the characteristics of Bear Markets in the list below:

Across

**[1]** Investors are not hopeful about the future.

**[3]** There is not much money to invest.

**[5]** It is expensive to borrow money.

**[6]** Companies are making less money.

**[10]** Prices are decreasing over a period of time.

Down

**[2]** People don't trust the people in charge.

**[4]** The market is changing a lot.

**[7]** The economy is not doing well and people don't have jobs.

**[8]** Investors are not hopeful about the market.

**[9]** Fewer people are buying and selling shares.

*See Solution on p. 191*

# Scramble Puzzle #5a - Trading Instruments

## Uncramble the Bull Market characteristics in the list below

EMIOONCC GTWROH

OMPTSIIM

OWL IENTSRET ERSTA

RSNIIG COAORRTPE PITOFRS

BLLISUH SIEEMNNTT

HHIG LLEVES FO LUIDQTIIY

CCEOFNINDE NI LHISADEERP

IESARNECD TINRADG VUOMLE

RINSIG TKSOC PCEIRS

RCEDEUD VLIIOTTALY

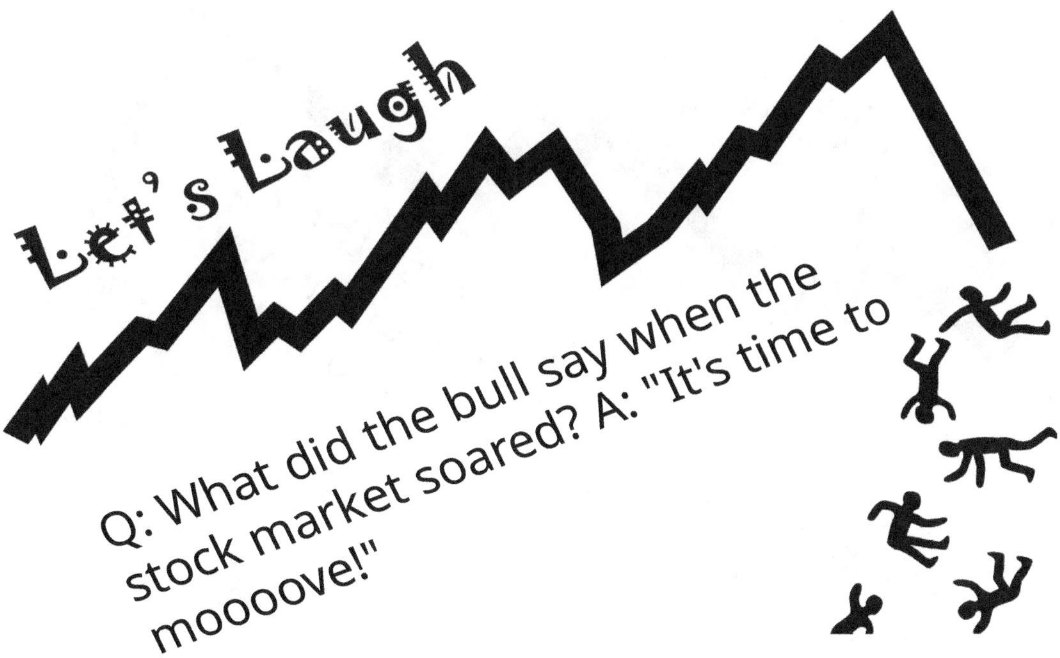


*See Solution on p. 191*

# Scramble Puzzle #5b - Trading Instruments

## Uncramble the Bear Market characteristics in the list below

EOMCINOC DLNCEIE

PMIISSESM

FLNLAIG CKSTO PCEIRS

RINSIG ITEESRNT SERTA

FLIANLG CAORTOPRE POITFRS

BISAREH SITEMNNET

OWL LLEEVS FO LQDIITIUY

IERESCAND VTAOIITLLY

DEAEERCSD TNRADIG VUOMLE

DRSISTUT NI LIERESADHP

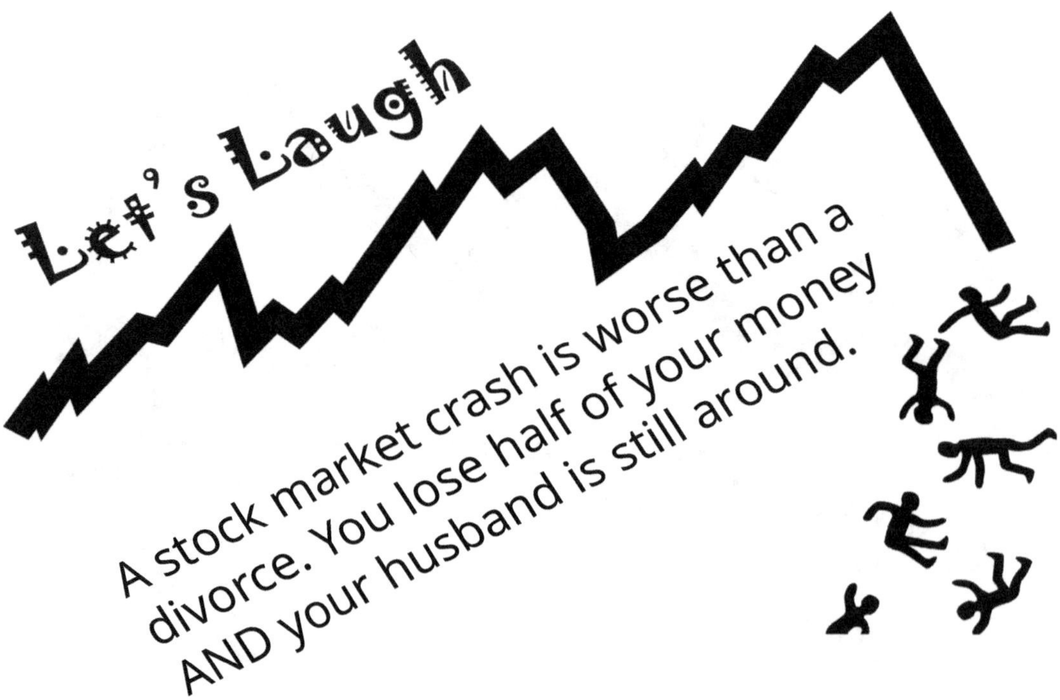


*See Solution on p. 191*

# Definition Match-Up #5a

## Bull Markets

### Associate the Bull Market characteristics to their Definitions

| | | | |
|---|---|---|---|
| 1 | Economic growth | A | The overall trend of the market is upward, with prices increasing for a sustained period of time. |
| 2 | Rising corporate profits | B | As prices rise, more investors are buying and selling shares, leading to higher trading volume. |
| 3 | Bullish sentiment | C | Investors are optimistic about the market and are more likely to invest in stocks. |
| 4 | Optimism about future growth | D | Often accompanied by a strong economy, with low unemployment and steady GDP growth. |
| 5 | Low interest rates | E | As the economy grows, companies tend to see increased profits, which can drive stock prices higher. |
| 6 | Rising stock prices | F | Low borrowing costs make it easier for companies to invest in growth and for individuals to buy homes and cars, leading to more economic activity. |
| 7 | Increased trading volume | G | Less volatile than bear markets, with less dramatic fluctuations in stock prices. |
| 8 | High levels of liquidity | H | Plenty of money is available to invest in the market, making it easy for investors to buy and sell shares. |
| 9 | Rising confidence in leadership | I | Investors have confidence in the leadership of companies and in the government's ability to manage the economy. |
| 10 | Reduced volatility | J | Investors are hopeful about the future of the economy and individual companies, which can drive stock prices higher. |

*See Solution on p. 192*

# Definition Match-Up #5b

Bear Markets

## Associate the Bear Market characteristics to their Definitions

| | | | |
|---|---|---|---|
| 1 | Increased volatility | A | The overall trend of the market is downward, with prices decreasing for a sustained period of time. |
| 2 | Economic decline | B | As prices fall, fewer investors are buying and selling shares, leading to lower trading volume. |
| 3 | Falling corporate profits | C | Investors are pessimistic about the market and are less likely to invest in stocks. |
| 4 | Rising interest rates | D | Often accompanied by a weak economy, with high unemployment and declining GDP. |
| 5 | Bearish sentiment | E | As the economy weakens, companies tend to see decreased profits, which can drive stock prices lower. |
| 6 | Decreased trading volume | F | Higher borrowing costs make it more difficult for companies to invest in growth and for individuals to buy homes and cars, leading to less economic activity. |
| 7 | Falling stock prices | G | More volatile than bull markets, with more dramatic fluctuations in stock prices. |
| 8 | Pessimism about future growth | H | Less money is available in the market, making it difficult for investors to buy and sell shares. |
| 9 | Falling confidence in leadership | I | Investors have less confidence in the leadership of companies and in the government's ability to manage the economy. |
| 10 | Low levels of liquidity | J | Investors are not hopeful about the future prospects of the economy and individual companies, which can drive stock prices lower. |

*See Solution on p. 192*

# Cloze Test #5a

## Fill In the Blanks Using Bull Market Characteristics below:

| Low interest rates - economic growth - bullish sentiment - optimism - Rising stock prices - rising corporate profits - increased trading volume - high levels of liquidity - rising confidence in leadership - reduced volatility |
|---|

Bear markets are often associated with a) ___________ and characterized by a sustained period of b) ___________. Companies tend to see c) ___________, which can further drive stock prices lower. Investors tend to have a d) ___________, meaning they are pessimistic about the market and less likely to invest in stocks. This e) ___________ is often fueled by a belief in the future decline of the economy and individual companies.

f) ___________ also play a role, making it more difficult for companies to invest in growth and for individuals to buy homes and cars, leading to less economic activity. Additionally, we see g) ___________ during a bear market, which is a sign of a weak market with h) ___________.

i) ___________, both in the leadership of companies and in the government's ability to manage the economy, contributes to the overall negative sentiment in the market. Bear markets tend to be more volatile with j) ___________, discouraging participation in the market.

*See Solution on p. 192*

# Cloze Test #5b

## Fill In the Blanks Using Bear Market Characteristics below:

| decreased trading volume - falling corporate profits - Rising interest rates - pessimism about future growth - Bearish sentiment - falling stock prices - economic decline - Falling confidence in leadership - low levels of liquidity - increased volatility |
|---|

Bear markets are often associated with a) ___________ and characterized by a sustained period of b) ___________. Companies tend to see c) ___________, which can further drive stock prices lower. Investors tend to have a d) ___________, meaning they are pessimistic about the market and less likely to invest in stocks. This e) ___________ is often fueled by a belief in the future decline of the economy and individual companies.

f) ___________ also play a role, making it more difficult for companies to invest in growth and for individuals to buy homes and cars, leading to less economic activity. Additionally, we see g) ___________ during a bear market, which is a sign of a weak market with h) ___________.

i) ___________, both in the leadership of companies and in the government's ability to manage the economy, contributes to the overall negative sentiment in the market. Bear markets tend to be more unstable with j) ___________, discouraging participation in the market.

*See Solution on p. 192*

# Missing Vowel #5a

## Learn about Bull Market Characteristics

| Puzzle | Clue |
| --- | --- |
| S T _ C K   P R _ C _ S   G _ _ N G   _ P | Prices are increasing over a period of time. |
| M _ R _   T R _ D _ N G | More people are buying and selling shares. |
| P _ S _ T _ V _   _ T T _ T _ D _ | Hopeful about the market. |
| _ C _ N _ M _ C   G R _ W T H | The economy is doing well and people have jobs. |
| C _ M P _ N _ _ S   M _ K _ N G   M _ R _   M _ N _ Y | Companies are more profitable. |
| L _ W   B _ R R _ W _ N G   C _ S T S | It is cheap to borrow money. |
| F _ W _ R   _ P S   _ N D   D _ W N S | The market is not changing as much. |
| P L _ N T Y   _ F   M _ N _ Y   T _   _ N V _ S T | There is a lot of money to invest. |
| L _ _ D _ R S H _ P   _ S   T R _ S T _ D | People trust the people in charge. |
| H _ P _   F _ R   T H _   F _ T _ R _ | Investors are hopeful about the future. |

*See Solution on p. 193*

# Missing Vowel #5b

## Learn about Bear Market Characteristics

| Puzzle | Clue |
|---|---|
| S T _ C K  P R _ C _ S  G _ _ N G  D _ W N | Prices are decreasing over a period of time. |
| L _ S S  T R _ D _ N G | Fewer people are buying and selling shares. |
| N _ G _ T _ V _  _ T T _ T _ D _ | Not hopeful about the market. |
| _ C _ N _ M _ C  D _ C L _ N _ | The economy is not doing well and people don't have jobs. |
| C _ M P _ N _ _ S  M _ K _ N G  L _ S S  M _ N _ Y | Companies are less profitable. |
| H _ G H  B _ R R _ W _ N G  C _ S T S | It is expensive to borrow money. |
| M _ R _  _ P S  _ N D  D _ W N S | The market is changing a lot. |
| L _ S S  M _ N _ Y  T _  _ N V _ S T | There is not much money to invest. |
| L _ _ D _ R S H _ P  _ S  N _ T  T R _ S T _ D | People don't trust the people in charge. |
| N _  H _ P _  F _ R  T H _  F _ T _ R _ | Investors are not hopeful about the future. |

*See Solution on p. 193*

# Double Puzzle #5a

**A list of words that describe characterictics of Bull Markets**

EOOIMNCC GTWROH

OSIMIPTM

OWL ITESENRT ASERT

RIINSG POTRFIS

BLSULIH SNIETNEMT

IHHG LDITIQUIY

RNIISG CDOINECFNE

TNIRDAG VUMLOE PU

RSINIG TCKOS PICERS

RUCEEDD VITLATOILY

B A B A B A A K , B A K A L L A A B L A M T T H E L E B E A M A K E T .

See Solution on p. 193

# Double Puzzle #5b

**A list of words that describe characterictics of Bear Markets**

PSESISMIM — 84 23 25 145 63

FNAILLG KCTSO PERICS — 33 47 137 74 98 / 71 31 75 9 / 73 51 67 55

RNIISG IENETSRT AESTR — 141 127 12 88 / 35 107 109 8 10 68 / 92 7 60 37 129

FIALNLG PTRIOFS — 119 76 46 136 42 / 85 4 20 19

BSRIEAH SNIEMTENT — 1 15 3 82 86 40 / 69 105 128 95 6 2 16 11

WLO LTIIQIDUY — 78 101 58 / 36 45 81 54 72

ICRSNEAED VIITOLTALY — 59 115 65 93 64 53 / 30 91 77 41 39 32 131 34 79

TDRINAG VUMLOE NDOW — 14 27 50 17 132 125 / 83 104 102 49 28 / 100 26 87

1 2 3 4 / 6 7 8 9 10 11 12 / 14 15 16 17 / 19 20 / B 23 (22 23) / 25 26 27 28

30 31 32 33 34 35 36 37 / 39 40 41 42 / B (44) 45 46 47 / 49 50 51 K (52) 53 54 55 , (56) / 58 59 60 H (61)

63 64 65 K (66) 67 68 69 / 71 72 73 74 75 76 77 78 79 / 81 82 83 84 85 86 87 88 / M (90) 91 92 93

95 H (96) A (97) 98 / 100 101 102 B (103) 104 105 / 107 H (108) 109 / A M O U (111 112 113 114) 115 T (116) / O (118) 119 / T H E (121 122 123) / 125 A (126) 127 128 129

131 132 / B U (134 135) 136 137 / M A (139 140) 141 K E T (142 143 144) 145 . (146)

See Solution on p. 193

## Cryptogram #5a - Characteristics of Bull Markets

| A | B | C | D | E | F | G | H | I | J | K | L | M | N | O | P | Q | R | S | T | U | V | W | X | Y | Z |
|---|---|---|---|---|---|---|---|---|---|---|---|---|---|---|---|---|---|---|---|---|---|---|---|---|---|
| | | | | | | | | | | | | | | | | | | | | | | | | | |

M B A A  R E I P Y F X  V S F Y U  A Y E J  F V

Y B W G V I H E  X W Y O B A E F H V U  E U J

R E I P Y F  M B M M A Y X  D G H O G  O E U

M Y  M V F G  J E U K Y I V B X  E U J

J E R E K H U K  D G Y U  F G Y L

Y Z Y U F B E A A L  M B I X F

*See Solution on p. 194*

# Cryptogram #5b - Characteristics of Bear Markets

| A | B | C | D | E | F | G | H | I | J | K | L | M | N | O | P | Q | R | S | T | U | V | W | X | Y | Z |
|---|---|---|---|---|---|---|---|---|---|---|---|---|---|---|---|---|---|---|---|---|---|---|---|---|---|
| | | | | | | | | | | | | | | | | | | | | | | | | | |

D K G Q    Z G Q B K A P    A S O N R S

L Y W W Y T N M A    Y E    A S K    P S O Q A A K Q Z

S G V K    D K K E    W O M M O J K L    D I

S Y R S K Q    Q K A N Q E P    Y E    A S K

P A O T B    Z G Q B K A    O V K Q    A S K

M O E R A K Q Z    G P    A S K    Z G Q B K A    S G P

G M J G I P    S Y P A O Q Y T G M M I

Q K T O V K Q K L    G E L    Q K G T S K L    E K J

S Y R S P

*See Solution on p. 194*

# Related Words Matching #5a

## Associate Characteristics of Bull Markets to their Related Words:

| | | | |
|---|---|---|---|
| 1 | Optimism | A | growth, revenue, earning, income, expanding margins |
| 2 | Low interest rates | B | expansion, development, prosperity, growth, expansion |
| 3 | Rising corporate profits | C | cheap credit, low borrowing costs, monetary easing, accommodative policy, loose monetary policy |
| 4 | Positive investor sentiment | D | bullish, optimism, confidence, positivity, trust |
| 5 | High levels of liquidity | E | positivity, hopefulness, confidence, assurance, faith |
| 6 | Rising confidence in leadership | F | trust, assurance, faith, belief, reliance |
| 7 | Increased trading volume | G | easy access, cash flow, cash rich, cash flow, high cash position |
| 8 | Rising stock prices | H | activity, liquidity, turnover, transaction, demand |
| 9 | Reduced volatility | I | appreciation, bull market, uptrend, growth, rally |
| 10 | Economic growth | J | stability, smoothness, less fluctuation, steady, calmness |

*See Solution on p. 194*

# Related Words  Matching #5b

## Associate Characteristics of Bear Markets to their Related Words:

| | | | |
|---|---|---|---|
| 1 | Pessimism | A | tight access, cash poor, cash crunch, lack of cash, low cash position |
| 2 | Falling stock prices | B | decline, revenue drop, loss, decrease in earning, shrinking margins |
| 3 | Rising interest rates | C | tight monetary policy, high borrowing costs, high credit, rate hike, monetary tightening |
| 4 | Falling corporate profits | D | negativity, skepticism, cynicism, despair, gloom |
| 5 | Negative investor sentiment | E | recession, downturn, contraction, decline, slump |
| 6 | Low levels of liquidity | F | depreciation, bear market, downtrend, decline, drop |
| 7 | Increased volatility | G | bearish, pessimism, skepticism, cynicism, lack of confidence |
| 8 | Decreased trading volume | H | instability, fluctuations, ups and downs, market swings, wild changes |
| 9 | Falling confidence in leadership | I | low activity, low liquidity, less transaction, low turnover, lack of demand |
| 10 | Economic decline | J | mistrust, doubt, uncertainty, lack of faith, lack of belief |

*See Solution on p. 194*

# Multiple-Choice Quiz #5a: Bull Market Characteristics

## Understanding Bull Market Characteristics

**Peter**: Hey Jane, have you been keeping up with the stock market lately?

**Jane**: Yeah, I've been following it pretty closely. Why do you ask?

**Peter**: Well, I've been hearing a lot of talk about a bull market and I'm not exactly sure what it means. Can you help me out?

**Jane**: Sure, a bull market is characterized by a sustained period of rising stock prices. It's usually accompanied by economic growth, rising corporate profits, and bullish sentiment among investors.

**Peter**: Got it. So what are some of the other indicators of a bull market?

**Jane**: Well, there's usually a lot of optimism about future growth, low interest rates, and increased trading volume. Plus, there's usually a lot of money available to invest in the market, which is known as high levels of liquidity.

**Peter**: That makes sense. And what about rising confidence in leadership? How does that factor in?

**Jane**: That's a good point. When investors have confidence in the leadership of companies and in the government's ability to manage the economy, it can contribute to the overall positive sentiment in the market and help drive stock prices higher.

**Peter**: And what about reduced volatility?

**Jane**: Right, bull markets tend to be less volatile than bear markets, meaning there are less dramatic fluctuations in stock prices. It makes it a more stable period for investors to make their investment decisions.

**Peter**: I see, so a bull market is generally a good time for investors.

**Jane**: Exactly, it's a great time to invest as the overall trend of the market is upward.

# Multiple-Choice Quiz #5a: Circle the Correct Answer

| | |
|---|---|
| 1. **What is a bull market characterized by?**<br>a) A sustained period of falling stock prices<br>b) A sustained period of rising stock prices<br>c) A period of stable stock prices<br>d) A period of high volatility | 2. **What are some indicators of a bull market?**<br>a) Economic decline and falling profits<br>b) High unemployment and declining GDP<br>c) Economic growth, rising corporate profits, and bullish sentiment among investors<br>d) High interest rates and low levels of liquidity |
| 3. **What is a common feature of bull markets?**<br>a) Pessimism about future growth<br>b) Optimism about future growth<br>c) Neutral sentiment about future growth<br>d) Fear of future growth | 4. **What is a benefit of low interest rates in a bull market?**<br>a) It is more difficult for companies to invest in growth<br>b) It is more difficult for individuals to buy homes and cars<br>c) It is easier for companies to invest in growth and for individuals to buy homes and cars<br>d) It has no effect on the market |
| 5. **What is a characteristic of bull markets in terms of volatility?**<br>a) More volatile than bear markets<br>b) Less volatile than bear markets<br>c) Same level of volatility as for bear markets<br>d) It depends on the market conditions | 6. **What is an indicator of high levels of liquidity in a bull market?**<br>a) Less money to invest in the market<br>b) The liquidity is low<br>c) There is no effect on liquidity<br>d) Plenty of money to invest in the market |
| 7. **What is the effect of rising confidence in leadership on a bull market?**<br>a) It reduces the overall positive sentiment<br>b) It contributes to the overall positive sentiment<br>c) It has no effect on the market<br>d) It causes investors to lose confidence | 8. **When is a good time to invest in a bull market?**<br>a) The overall trend of the market is upward<br>b) The overall trend of the market is downward<br>c) When the market is stable<br>d) When the market is volatile |
| 9. **What is a benefit of reduced volatility in a bull market?**<br>a) It makes it more difficult for investors to make investment decisions<br>b) More dramatic fluctuations in stock prices<br>c) It has no effect on the market<br>d) It makes it easier for investors to make investment decisions | 10. **What is the opposite of a bull market?**<br>a) A bear market<br>b) A stable market<br>c) A bull market<br>d) A neutral market |

*See Solution on p. 195*

# Multiple-Choice Quiz #5b: Bear Market Characteristics

## Understanding Bear Market Characteristics

- **Peter**: Hey Jane, have you been keeping up with the stock market lately?

- **Jane**: Yeah, I've been following it pretty closely. Why do you ask?

- **Peter**: Well, I've been hearing a lot of talk about a bear market and I'm not exactly sure what it means. Can you help me out?

- **Jane**: Sure, a bear market is characterized by a sustained period of falling stock prices. It's usually accompanied by economic decline, falling corporate profits, and bearish sentiment among investors.

- **Peter**: Got it. So what are some of the other indicators of a bear market?

- **Jane**: Well, there's usually a lot of pessimism about future growth, rising interest rates, and decreased trading volume. Plus, there's usually less money available to invest in the market, which is known as low levels of liquidity.

- **Peter**: That makes sense. And what about falling confidence in leadership? How does that factor in?

- **Jane**: That's a good point. When investors have less confidence in the leadership of companies and in the government's ability to manage the economy, it can contribute to the overall negative sentiment in the market and help drive stock prices lower.

- **Peter**: And what about increased volatility?

- **Jane**: Right, bear markets tend to be more volatile than bull markets, meaning there are more dramatic fluctuations in stock prices. It makes it a more risky period for investors to make their investment decisions.

- **Peter**: I see, so a bear market is generally a bad time for investors.

- **Jane**: Exactly, it's a risky time to invest as the overall trend of the market is downward.

# Multiple-Choice Quiz #5b: Circle the Correct Answer

| | |
|---|---|
| 1. **What is a bear market characterized by?**<br>a) A sustained period of rising stock prices<br>b) A period of stable stock prices<br>c) A sustained period of falling stock prices<br>d) A period of low volatility | 2. **What are some indicators of a bear market?**<br>a) Economic growth, rising corporate profits, and bullish sentiment among investors<br>b) Economic decline, falling corporate profits, and bearish sentiment among investors<br>c) High unemployment and declining GDP<br>d) High interest rates and low levels of liquidity |
| 3. **What is a characteristic of bear markets in terms of volatility?**<br>a) It depends on the market conditions<br>b) They tend to be less volatile than bull markets<br>c) They have the same level of volatility as bull markets<br>d) They tend to be more volatile than bull markets | 4. **What is a challenge of rising interest rates in a bear market?**<br>a) It is more difficult for companies to invest in growth<br>b) It is more difficult for individuals to buy homes and cars<br>c) It is easier for companies to invest in growth and for individuals to buy homes and cars<br>d) It has no effect on the market |
| 5. **What is a characteristic of bull markets in terms of volatility?**<br>a) More volatile than bear markets<br>b) Less volatile than bear markets<br>c) Same level of volatility as for bear markets<br>d) It depends on the market conditions | 6. **What is an indicator of low levels of liquidity in a bear market?**<br>a) Less money is available to invest<br>b) Plenty of money is available to invest<br>c) There is no effect on liquidity<br>d) The liquidity is high |
| 7. **What is the effect of falling confidence in leadership on a bear market?**<br>a) It has no effect on the market<br>b) It reduces the overall negative sentiment c) It contributes to the overall negative sentiment<br>d) It causes investors to have more confidence | 8. **When is a risky time to invest in a bear market?**<br>a) The overall trend of the market is downward<br>b) The overall trend of the market is upward<br>c) When the market is stable<br>d) When the market is volatile |
| 9. **What is a challenge of decreased trading volume in a bear market?**<br>a) More dramatic fluctuations in stock prices<br>b) Easier for investors to buy and sell shares<br>c) It has no effect on the market<br>d) More difficult for investors to buy and sell shares | 10. **What is the opposite of a bear market?**<br>a) A bull market<br>b) A stable market<br>c) A bear market<br>d) A neutral market |

*See Solution on p. 195*

# Unit 6: Fundamental Analysis

Fundamental analysis is a method of evaluating stocks by looking at a company's financial and economic fundamentals. It is a way to determine a company's intrinsic value and assess its growth potential. Imagine you are considering buying a stock, but you want to make sure it's a good investment. With fundamental analysis, you can look at a company's financial statements and see how much money it's making, how much debt it has, and how well it's managed. By understanding these things, you can make a more informed decision about whether to buy or sell the stock. It's like being a detective, but instead of solving a crime, you're solving the mystery of a company's financial health. It's a way to find the hidden gems in the stock market and make better investment decisions.

For example, if a company has strong revenue and earnings growth, and a healthy balance sheet, it may be a good investment. On the other hand, if a company is struggling financially, it may be a riskier investment.

It's important to note that fundamental analysis is not a surefire way to pick winning stocks, as there are many factors that can influence a stock's performance, and some of them are hard to predict. But it can be a useful tool to help you make more informed investment decisions.

Overall, fundamental analysis is all about looking at a company's financials and determining whether it is a good investment at its current stock price. If a company looks financially strong and is undervalued according to the valuation metrics, then it may be a good buy for an investor. On the other hand, if a company looks financially weak and is overvalued, it may not be a good investment.

# Fundamental Analysis: Key Concepts

## Key Concepts of Fundamental Analysis

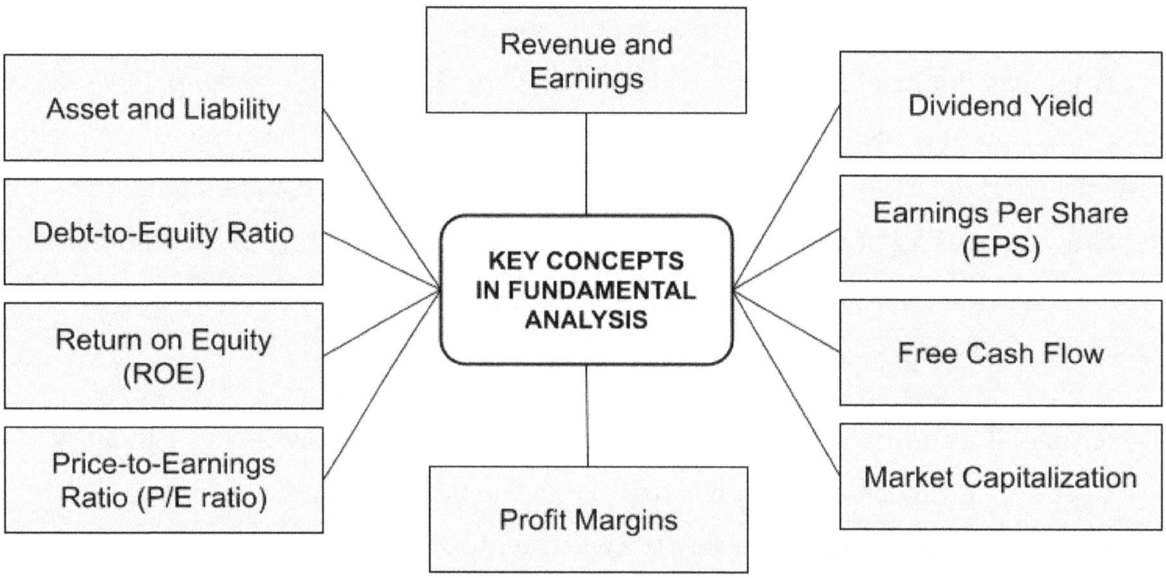


Don't worry if the main key concepts of fundamental analysis seem hard to understand at first. Don't let financial jargon scare you. With time and continuous exposure to these new terms, you will soon understand them and, with practice, be able to use them more easily in conversations.

Acquiring new vocabulary may take some time, but it is a valuable and fulfilling experience. Practice makes perfect, and the same applies to learning new vocabulary. Be patient. Consistent repetition will help solidify new terms and concepts in your mind.

# Fundamental Analysis: Key Concepts

## Key Concepts of Fundamental Analysis

### Fundamental Analysis

- **Revenue and Earnings:** A company's financial performance and future growth potential are shown by its revenue and earnings.
- **Profit Margins:** A measure of a company's profitability, calculated by dividing net income by revenue.
- **Asset and Liability:** A company's resources and debt levels are shown by its assets and liabilities.
- **Debt-to-Equity Ratio:** A measure of a company's leverage (using other people's money to invest), compares total liabilities to total equity.
- **Return on Equity (ROE):** A measure of a company's profitability from shareholders' investments.
- **Price-to-Earnings Ratio (P/E ratio):** A measure of a company's valuation, compares stock price to earnings per share.
- **Dividend Yield:** A measure of dividends paid to shareholders relative to stock price.
- **Earnings Per Share (EPS):** A measure of a company's profitability, calculated by dividing net income by outstanding shares.
- **Free Cash Flow:** Cash generated after accounting for capital expenditures, important for paying dividends or investing in growth.
- **Market Capitalization:** The total value of a company's outstanding shares, used to classify companies by size.

# Word Search Puzzle #6 - Fundamental Analysis

## Find the Key Concepts of Fundamental Analysis in the list below:

| K | A | N | Q | U | V | P | I | K | F | T | A | B | S | T | M | X | X | F | X |
|---|---|---|---|---|---|---|---|---|---|---|---|---|---|---|---|---|---|---|---|
| J | H | R | F | R | J | H | W | R | D | V | X | L | F | F | X | M | K | Y | O |
| C | Z | F | E | E | G | F | F | R | E | E | C | A | S | H | F | L | O | W | G |
| D | E | B | T | T | O | E | Q | U | I | T | Y | R | A | T | I | O | M | Q | Z |
| G | S | S | H | X | U | X | G | O | Q | O | W | H | X | L | D | Y | U | V | J |
| A | C | S | F | M | H | R | P | R | O | F | I | T | M | A | R | G | I | N | S |
| F | D | I | V | I | D | E | N | D | Y | I | E | L | D | U | Q | Q | E | G | W |
| C | S | S | Y | V | L | T | T | O | D | F | Y | U | B | X | F | A | W | M | L |
| D | G | L | Z | B | H | W | G | O | N | X | G | V | S | T | P | Q | U | C | U |
| R | J | W | K | Q | P | B | K | Y | R | E | U | U | Z | W | F | Y | A | M | D |
| C | R | U | K | F | B | U | S | K | J | B | Q | V | V | S | R | Z | C | I | D |
| N | Z | E | Z | Z | M | O | D | K | T | N | U | U | G | U | X | H | N | V | E |
| M | A | R | K | E | T | C | A | P | I | T | A | L | I | Z | A | T | I | O | N |
| T | J | N | P | I | R | O | A | Y | Q | U | X | U | P | T | P | Q | X | Z | T |
| O | N | K | G | D | L | K | Q | J | M | G | S | X | P | Z | Y | G | K | R | T |
| L | D | H | F | J | S | C | C | C | K | J | Y | W | U | P | I | D | T | N | R |
| C | S | A | S | S | E | T | A | N | D | L | I | A | B | I | L | I | T | Y | U |
| R | E | V | E | N | U | E | A | N | D | E | A | R | N | I | N | G | S | B | F |
| K | E | A | R | N | I | N | G | S | P | E | R | S | H | A | R | E | E | W | R |
| P | R | I | C | E | T | O | E | A | R | N | I | N | G | S | R | A | T | I | O |

ASSET AND LIABILITY
EARNINGS PER SHARE
PRICE-TO-EARNINGS RATIO
REVENUE AND EARNINGS
DEBT-TO-EQUITY RATIO
FREE CASH FLOW
PROFIT MARGINS
DIVIDEND YIELD
MARKET CAPITALIZATION
RETURN ON EQUITY

*See Solution on p. 195*

# Learn about Fundamental Analysis

Across

**[1]** A company's financial performance and future growth potential are shown by its revenue and earnings.

**[3]** A company's resources and debt levels are shown by its assets and liabilities.

**[4]** A measure of a company's leverage, compares total liabilities to total equity.

**[5]** (ROE) A measure of a company's profitability from shareholders' investments.

**[10]** The total value of a company's outstanding shares, used to classify companies by size.

Down

**[2]** A measure of a company's profitability, calculated by dividing net income by revenue.

**[6]** (P/E ratio) A measure of a company's valuation, compares stock price to earnings per share.

**[7]** A measure of dividends paid to shareholders relative to stock price.

**[8]** (EPS) A measure of a company's profitability, calculated by dividing net income by outstanding shares.

**[9]** Cash generated after accounting for capital expenditures, important for paying dividends or investing in growth.

*See Solution on p. 195*

# Scramble Puzzle #6 - Fundamental Analysis

## Uncramble the different key concepts in the list below

POFIRT MGNRAIS

RRETUN NO EITUQY

TESAS DAN LLIIBATIY

EIGNRANS RPE HAESR

PIN-AEEGONCIR-RTS AORTI

EERF AHCS OWLF

DO-IBTUTQTEE-Y ORATI

REUNVEE NDA ENNIGRAS

MKAERT CZLIAPIOTTIAAN

DNEVIIDD IEDYL

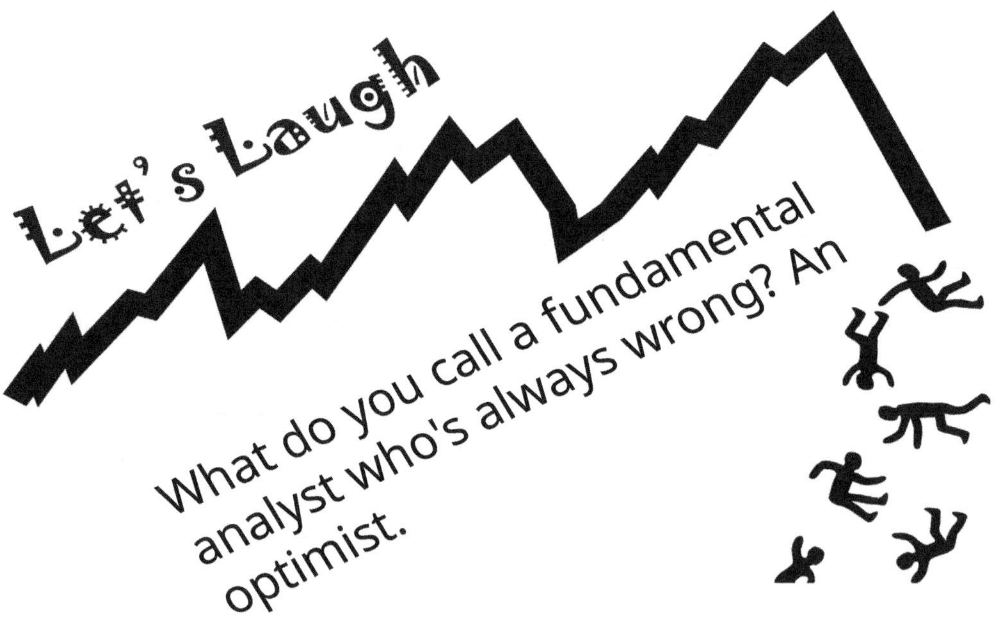


*See Solution on p. 196*

# Definition Match-Up #6

## Fundamental Analysis

### Associate the *Key Concepts* to their Definition

| | | | |
|---|---|---|---|
| **1** | Earnings Per Share (EPS) | **A** | A company's financial performance and future growth potential are shown by its revenue and earnings. |
| **2** | Price-to-Earnings Ratio (P/E ratio) | **B** | A measure of a company's profitability, calculated by dividing net income by revenue. |
| **3** | Asset and Liability | **C** | A company's resources and debt levels are shown by its assets and liabilities. |
| **4** | Revenue and Earnings | **D** | A measure of a company's leverage, compares total liabilities to total equity. |
| **5** | Profit Margins | **E** | A measure of a company's profitability from shareholders' investments. |
| **6** | Free Cash Flow | **F** | A measure of a company's valuation, compares stock price to earnings per share. |
| **7** | Market Capitalization | **G** | A measure of dividends paid to shareholders relative to stock price. |
| **8** | Return on Equity (ROE) | **H** | A measure of a company's profitability, calculated by dividing net income by outstanding shares. |
| **9** | Debt-to-Equity Ratio | **I** | Cash generated after accounting for capital expenditures, important for paying dividends or investing in growth. |
| **10** | Dividend Yield | **J** | The total value of a company's outstanding shares, used to classify companies by size. |

*See Solution on p. 196*

# Cloze Test #6

## Fill In the Blanks Using the Key Concepts below:

Profit margins - Free cash flow - Market capitalization -
Asset and liability - Return on equity (ROE) - Debt-to-equity ratio -
Dividend yield - Revenue and earnings - Earnings per share (EPS) -
Price-to-earnings ratio (P/E ratio)

Fundamental analysis can use many metrics to measure a company's financial performance. a) ___________ show how much money the company brings in and makes. b) ___________ show how much money the company keeps as profit after paying expenses. c) ___________ show what the company owns and what it owes. d) ___________ shows how much debt the company has compared to its equity. e) ___________ (ROE) shows how much profit the company makes compared to shareholder's investment. f) ___________ (P/E ratio) compares the stock price to the earnings per share and tells if the stock is overvalued or undervalued. g) ___________ shows how much money the company pays to shareholders as a percentage of stock price. h) ___________ shows how much profit is made per share of stock. i) ___________ shows how much cash the company has left after expenses and investments. j) ___________ shows the total value of the company's stock. By understanding these metrics, investors can make informed decisions about investing in a company.

*See Solution on p. 196*

# Missing Vowel #6

## Learn about Fundamental Analysis

| Puzzle | Clue |
|---|---|
| P R _ F _ T   M _ R G _ N S | A measure of a company's profitability, calculated by dividing net income by revenue. |
| _ S S _ T   _ N D   L _ _ B _ L _ T Y | A company's resources and debt levels are shown by its assets and liabilities. |
| D _ B T - T _ - _ Q _ _ T Y   R _ T _ _ | A measure of a company's leverage, compares total liabilities to total equity. |
| R _ T _ R N   _ N   _ Q _ _ T Y | (ROE) A measure of a company's profitability from shareholders' investments. |
| P R _ C _ - T _ - _ _ R N _ N G S   R _ T _ _ | (P/E ratio) A measure of a company's valuation, compares stock price to earnings per share. |
| D _ V _ D _ N D   Y _ _ L D | A measure of dividends paid to shareholders relative to stock price. |
| _ _ R N _ N G S   P _ R   S H _ R _ | (EPS) A measure of a company's profitability, calculated by dividing net income by outstanding shares. |
| F R _ _   C _ S H   F L _ W | Cash generated after accounting for capital expenditures, important for paying dividends or investing in growth. |
| M _ R K _ T   C _ P _ T _ L _ Z _ T _ _ N | The total value of a company's outstanding shares, used to classify companies by size. |
| R _ V _ N _ _   _ N D   _ _ R N _ N G S | A company's financial performance and future growth potential are shown by its revenue and earnings. |

*See Solution on p. 196*

# Double Puzzle #6

## A list of words that describe concepts of Fundamental Analysis

ERNIGANS ERP HERSA

PNEONI-A-CGERRTIS IRAOT

ESATS DAN LBTAIIILY

RVUEENE NDA EGIRANNS

POFIRT MGINARS

REFE HCAS WOFL

MKERAT CLAZIIAPAITOTN

RTUREN NO EITUQY

DETIOBTQ-ET-UY IRAOT

DDNEVIID LEYDI

See Solution on p. 197

## Cryptogram #6 - An Essential Requirement of Fundamental Analysis

| A | B | C | D | E | F | G | H | I | J | K | L | M | N | O | P | Q | R | S | T | U | V | W | X | Y | Z |
|---|---|---|---|---|---|---|---|---|---|---|---|---|---|---|---|---|---|---|---|---|---|---|---|---|---|
| | | | | | | | | | | | | | | | | | | | | | | | | | |

S M O T L Q A O N L B    L O L B K I V I    J S N A O

R A W M V R A I    X L N V A O F A    L O T    L

B J O H N A R Q    J M N B J J Y    L I    V N    V I

O J N    L B E L K I    X J I I V U B A    N J

X R A T V F N    N P A    I P J R N N A R Q    X R V F A

Q J C A Q A O N I    J S    L    I N J F Y

*See Solution on p. 197*

# Related Words Matching #6

## Associate Concepts of Fundamental Analysis to their Related Words:

| | | | |
|---|---|---|---|
| 1 | Earnings Per Share (EPS) | A | sales, income, billing, turnover, gross income |
| 2 | Price-to-Earnings Ratio (P/E ratio) | B | gross margin, operating margin, net margin, return on sales, profitability |
| 3 | Profit Margins | C | property, equity, investments, inventory, cash |
| 4 | Free Cash Flow | D | leverage, financial leverage, indebtedness, creditworthiness, solvency |
| 5 | Asset and Liability | E | return on assets, return on capital, return on investment, return on net assets, return on shareholder's equity |
| 6 | Return on Equity (ROE) | F | valuation, price-to-book, price-to-sales, forward P/E, price-to-cash flow |
| 7 | Debt-to-Equity Ratio | G | payout, dividend coverage, payout ratio, yield, dividends |
| 8 | Market Capitalization | H | net income, profit, earnings, diluted EPS, basic EPS |
| 9 | Dividend Yield | I | operating cash flow, net cash flow, free cash flow per share, cash flow from operations, cash flow |
| 10 | Revenue and Earnings | J | valuation, market cap, market value, capitalization, market size |

*See Solution on p. 197*

# Multiple-Choice Quiz #6: Concepts of Fundamental Analysis

### Fundamental Analysis Analogies

- **Patrick**: Hey Emma, I heard you're trying to learn more about fundamental analysis in the stock market. Can I help you with anything?
- **Emma**: Hi Patrick, yes please! I'm trying to understand some of the basic concepts, like revenue and earnings. Can you explain it to me?
- **Patrick**: Sure thing. Revenue and earnings are like a farmer's harvest. Just like a farmer works hard all year to grow crops and bring in a harvest, a company works hard to bring in revenue and earn profits.
- **Emma**: Oh, I see. That makes sense. How about profit margins?
- **Patrick**: Profit margins are like a chef's recipe. Just like a chef carefully measures ingredients to create the perfect dish, a company carefully manages its expenses to maintain a healthy profit margin.
- **Emma**: Interesting analogy. And what about assets and liabilities?
- **Patrick**: Assets and liabilities are like a person's bank account. Just like a person has money in their account and debts they owe, a company has assets it owns and liabilities it owes.
- **Emma**: Okay, I understand. How about the debt-to-equity ratio?
- **Patrick**: The debt-to-equity ratio is like a person's credit score. Just like a person's credit score tells how much they owe compared to how much credit they have, a company's debt-to-equity ratio tells how much debt it has compared to its equity.
- **Emma**: Got it. Thanks, Patrick. Can you explain the return on equity?
- **Patrick**: Return on equity is like a savings account interest. Just like a savings account earns interest on the money deposited, a company earns a return on the equity invested by shareholders.
- **Emma**: That's helpful. What about the P/E ratio?
- **Patrick**: The P/E ratio is like a real estate value. Just like the value of a house is determined by its price and the income it generates, the value of a stock is determined by its price and the earnings of the company.
- **Emma**: I see. And the dividend yield?
- **Patrick**: The dividend yield is like a rental property income. Just like a rental property generates income for the owner, a company's dividend yield generates income for its shareholders.
- **Emma**: This is all really helpful, Patrick. Thank you so much.
- **Patrick**: No problem, Emma. I'm happy to help. And remember, always keep learning and practicing, soon you'll be a pro in no time!
- **Emma**: I will, thanks again!

# Multiple-Choice Quiz #6: Concepts of Fundamental Analysis

| | |
|---|---|
| 1. **According to the analogy, what does a company's revenue and earnings represent?**<br>a) A farmer's hard work throughout the year<br>b) A chef's precision in measuring ingredients<br>c) Money in a person's bank account<br>d) Interest earned on a savings account | 2. **How does the analogy "Profit margins are like a chef's recipe" describe a company's expenses management?**<br>a) Like a chef who creates the perfect dish<br>b) Like a farmer working hard for the harvest<br>c) Like a person who manages their debts<br>d) Like an interest earned on equity invested |
| 3. **How does the analogy "Assets and liabilities are like a person's bank account" illustrates a company's financial standing?**<br>a) Company money and debts it owes<br>b) A company works hard to bring in a harvest<br>c) A company carefully measures ingredients to maintain a healthy profit margin<br>d) A company earns a return on the equity invested by shareholders | 4. **What does "Debt-to-equity ratio is like a person's credit score" suggest about a company's financial leverage?**<br>a) How much return a company earns on the equity invested by shareholders<br>b) Value of a stock based on price and earnings<br>c) The income generated by a rental property<br>d) How much a company owes compared to how much credit it has |
| 5. **How is a company's return on equity described in the analogy "Return on equity is like a savings account interest"?**<br>a) Like interest earned in a savings account<br>b) Like a chef's recipe for a good profit margin<br>c) Like a person's bank account balance<br>d) Like a house generating income | 6. **According to the analogy, what does the P/E ratio represent for a stock?**<br>a) Interest from a savings account<br>b) Value of a stock based on price and earnings<br>c) Income generated by a rental property<br>d) A company's debt compared to its equity |
| 7. **How does the analogy "Dividend yield is like a rental property income" describe a company's returns to shareholders?**<br>a) Like income from a rental property<br>b) Like a chef's recipe for a good profit margin<br>c) Like a person's credit score<br>d) Like interest earned in a savings account. | 8. **According to the analogy, what does a company's revenue and earnings represent?**<br>a) Interest earned on a savings account<br>b) A chef's precision in measuring ingredients<br>c) Money in a person's bank account<br>d) A farmer's hard work throughout the year |
| 9. **What does the analogy "Profit margins are like a chef's recipe" suggest about a company's financial management?**<br>a) The focus is on creating the perfect dish<br>b) The focus is on bringing in a harvest<br>c) The company is carefully measuring expenses to maintain a healthy profit margin<br>d) The return on the equity invested by shareholders | 10. **How does the analogy "Assets and liabilities are like a person's bank account" illustrate a company's financial standing?**<br>a) A company is carefully measuring expenses to maintain a healthy profit margin<br>b) The focus is on bringing in a harvest<br>c) Company assets and the liabilities it owes<br>d) A company is earning a return on the equity invested by shareholders |

*See Solution on p. 197*

# Unit 7: Technical Analysis

Have you ever wondered how investors predict the future movements of stock prices? One popular method is called technical analysis. This approach involves studying charts and historical data to identify patterns and trends that can indicate when to buy or sell a stock. Unlike fundamental analysis, which looks at a company's financial and economic factors, technical analysis focuses solely on the market's price and volume data. It's a fascinating way to gain insights into the stock market and make informed investment decisions.

Technical analysis is a method used by traders and investors to study the past performance of a stock, currency, commodity or any other traded instrument, in order to predict its future movements. It's like trying to see patterns in a stock's price and trading volume. For example, if a stock's price has been going up for a while, and a lot of people are buying it, it might keep going up. Or if the price has been going down and not many people are buying, it might keep going down. It is based on the idea that market trends, as shown by charts and other technical indicators, tend to repeat themselves.

The basic assumption of technical analysis is that the market discounts everything and that the price reflects all the fundamental and technical factors that influence it. Technical analysts believe that by studying charts and historical data, they can identify patterns and trends that can indicate when to buy or sell a stock.

It's important to keep in mind that technical analysis is not an exact science and that no single approach or indicator can guarantee success. Furthermore, it should not be used in isolation but rather in conjunction with other analysis tools and fundamental analysis.

# Technical Analysis: Key Concepts

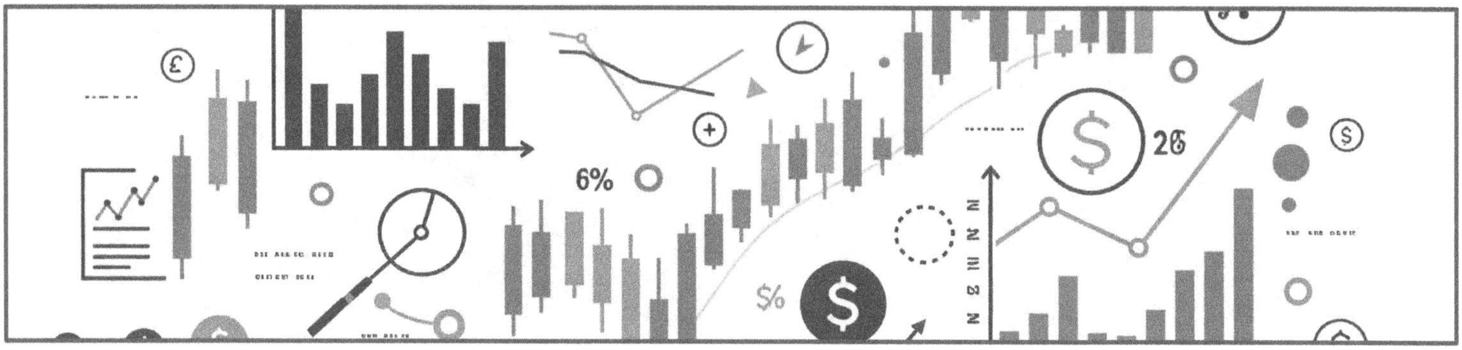

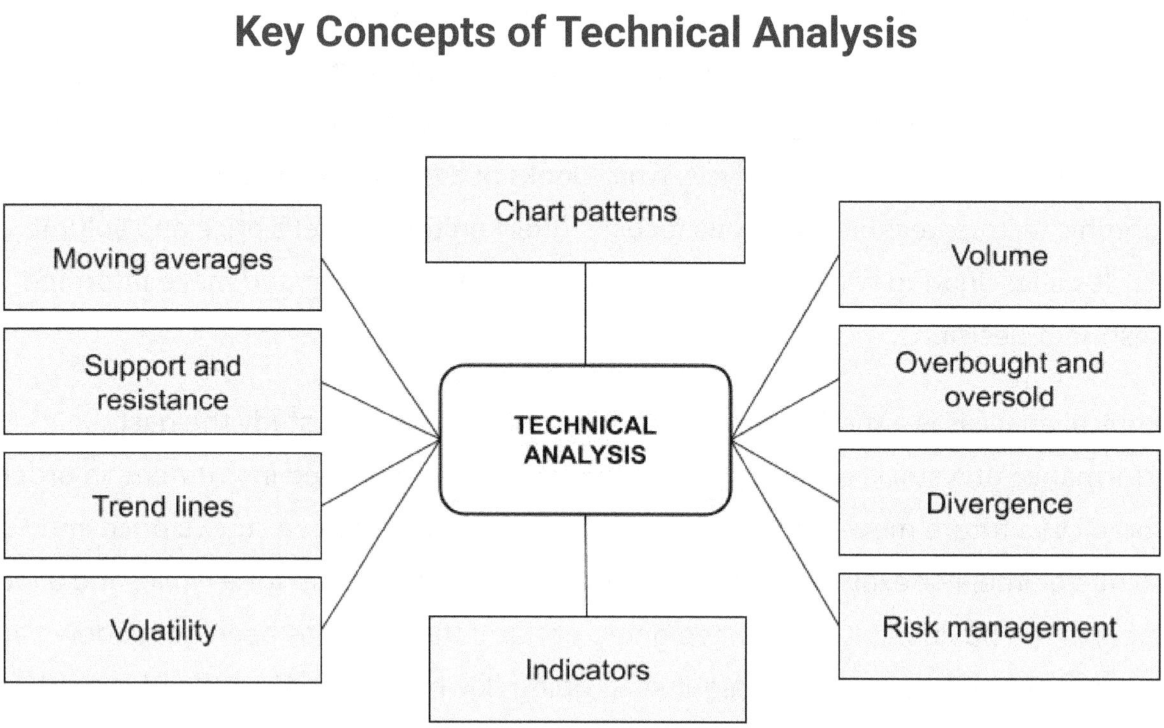


The reliability of technical analysis can be a matter of debate among traders and investors. Some traders swear by it and use it as the sole basis for their trading decisions, while others dismiss it as unreliable or even fraudulent.

In any case, learning about technical analysis can be helpful for ESL business students by providing them with a valuable tool for understanding and analyzing financial markets, developing analytical and critical thinking skills, and becoming more informed investors, entrepreneurs and consumers.

# Technical Analysis: Key Concepts

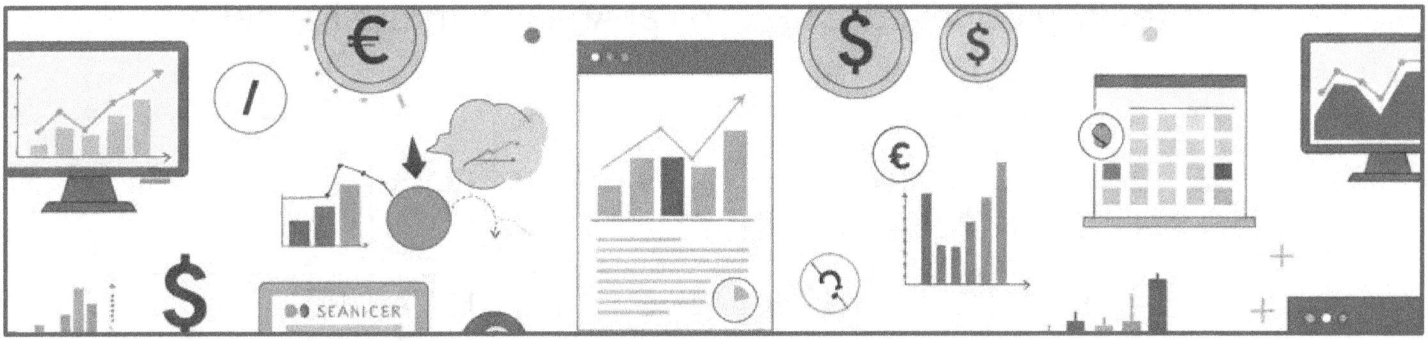

## Key Concepts of Technical Analysis

| Technical Analysis |
|---|
| • **Chart patterns**: The study of past price and volume data in the form of charts to identify patterns such as head and shoulders, double tops, and triangles, which can indicate a change in trend.<br>• **Indicators**: Mathematical calculations based on the price and/or volume of a stock, such as the Relative Strength Index (RSI) and Moving Average Convergence Divergence (MACD), used to generate buy and sell signals.<br>• **Moving averages**: A way to smooth out data and identify trends by calculating the average price over a certain period of time.<br>• **Support and resistance**: The levels at which a stock's price tends to stop rising or falling, and may change direction.<br>• **Trend lines**: A straight line that connects two or more price points and is used to identify a current trend in the market.<br>• **Volatility**: The degree of variation in a stock's price, used to measure market risk and potential profit.<br>• **Volume**: The number of shares or contracts traded in a given period, used to confirm trends and indicate market strength or weakness.<br>• **Overbought and oversold**: Conditions in which a stock's price has risen or fallen too far too fast and may be due for a correction.<br>• **Divergence**: A difference between the direction of a stock's price and that of an indicator, which may signal a change in trend.<br>• **Risk management**: A set of techniques to control and minimize the potential losses and maximize the potential gains of a trade. |

# Word Search Puzzle #7 - Technical Analysis

## Find the Key Concepts of Technical Analysis in the list below:

| P | E | D | J | X | F | X | E | X | I | P | N | K | R | I | C | O | H | J | R | E |
|---|---|---|---|---|---|---|---|---|---|---|---|---|---|---|---|---|---|---|---|---|
| R | J | S | I | H | M | W | R | J | Y | D | U | B | P | Q | K | I | V | M | E | T |
| I | D | I | R | J | Y | X | C | R | Q | S | F | W | T | I | E | D | B | A | V | R |
| C | E | E | A | R | N | I | N | G | S | P | E | R | S | H | A | R | E | R | E | F |
| E | B | H | V | K | D | I | Q | B | H | N | W | X | A | C | M | Y | N | K | N | J |
| T | T | O | N | P | N | I | J | B | Z | L | V | U | Z | G | T | C | G | E | U | R |
| O | T | J | I | A | U | N | V | M | P | Z | T | Y | S | I | L | Y | Q | T | E | P |
| E | O | L | D | M | Z | O | K | I | U | Q | S | W | L | Y | T | O | G | C | A | R |
| A | E | G | Z | R | F | M | S | D | D | K | F | I | Z | I | O | V | I | A | N | O |
| R | Q | E | S | J | C | R | T | W | R | E | B | A | U | O | V | B | V | P | D | F |
| N | U | Q | I | P | K | U | E | X | V | A | N | Q | P | E | Y | Y | N | I | E | I |
| I | I | Z | M | C | X | V | G | E | I | H | E | D | W | X | S | A | N | T | A | T |
| N | T | K | O | B | F | Y | G | L | C | N | K | X | Y | Z | B | J | N | A | R | M |
| G | Y | U | Y | W | P | H | D | N | O | A | A | R | K | I | N | D | Z | L | N | A |
| S | R | W | U | L | H | N | E | N | Q | B | S | D | A | P | E | E | H | I | I | R |
| R | A | A | J | Y | A | K | R | I | E | R | H | H | S | W | S | L | Q | Z | N | G |
| A | T | C | S | T | L | U | E | B | D | Y | H | D | F | E | S | R | D | A | G | I |
| T | I | C | E | Z | T | U | B | S | B | E | S | P | L | L | P | Z | S | T | S | N |
| I | O | S | C | E | X | B | N | R | D | X | K | M | W | F | O | Y | F | I | O | S |
| O | S | Q | R | B | U | E | W | G | W | L | H | Z | K | C | O | W | G | O | J | Q |
| A | E | N | R | H | W | G | T | O | B | L | Q | M | S | R | Z | O | E | N | I | Q |

ASSET AND LIABILITY
DIVIDEND YIELD
FREE CASH FLOW
PRICE-TO-EARNINGS RATIO
RETURN ON EQUITY

DEBT-TO-EQUITY RATIO
EARNINGS PER SHARE
MARKET CAPITALIZATION
PROFIT MARGINS
REVENUE AND EARNINGS

*See Solution on p. 198*

# Crossword Puzzle #7

## Learn about Technical Analysis

Across

**[2]** Tools guiding stock buying or selling decisions.

**[3]** Filters aiding clearer stock trend perception.

**[4]** Price boundaries for stocks' high or low limits.

**[9]** Discrepancy between stock price and trend-change indicator.

**[10]** Controlling losses and maximizing gains in trading.

Down

**[1]** Analyzing stock charts to spot trend-change patterns.

**[5]** Connects price points to display the current stock trend.

**[6]** Measures stock price fluctuations.

**[7]** Indicates market sentiment toward a stock.

**[8]** Occurs when a stock's price changes too rapidly.

*See Solution on p. 198*

# Scramble Puzzle #7 - Technical Analysis

**Uncramble the different key concepts in the list below**

EDNRT NLSIE

OBRVUHGOET

OERSOLVD

VUOMLE

IIARONCDTS

DEERVNGCIE

MNIOVG AEVAGERS

SORPPUT

RCNSSAETIE

VLAITLITOY

RCHTA PEARNTTS

*See Solution on p. 198*

# Definition Match-Up #7

## Technical Analysis

### Associate the *Key Concepts* to their Definition

| | | | |
|---|---|---|---|
| **1** | Overbought and oversold | **A** | Bouncy castle limits on how high or low a stock's price can go. |
| **2** | Indicators | **B** | Indicator of market sentiment towards a stock, like a crowd at a concert. |
| **3** | Divergence | **C** | A safety net for trading, to control and minimize potential losses and maximize potential gains. |
| **4** | Chart patterns | **D** | A stock's price that's risen or fallen too fast, like a bargain sale. |
| **5** | Volume | **E** | Navigational tools that give directions on when to buy or sell a stock. |
| **6** | Trend lines | **F** | A measure of a company's valuation, compares stock price to earnings per share. |
| **7** | Support and resistance | **G** | Connecting price points like dots to show the stock's current trend. |
| **8** | Volatility | **H** | A smoothing filter that helps see the stock's trend more clearly. |
| **9** | Moving averages | **I** | Reading stock charts like a book, to identify patterns that indicate a change in trend. |
| **10** | Risk management | **J** | The total value of a company's outstanding shares, used to classify companies by size. |

*See Solution on p. 198*

# Cloze Test #7

## Fill In the Blanks Using the Key Concepts below:

| Overbought and oversold - Volume - Divergence - Volatility - Risk management - Indicators - Trend lines - Support and resistance - Chart patterns - Moving averages |
|---|

To succeed in the stock market, it is important to understand the most common technical analysis terms.

a) ____________________ are tools that traders use to analyze the market and predict future price movements. b) ____________________ are a type of indicator that smooths out price data by creating a constantly updated average price. c) ____________________ are recognizable shapes that occur on price charts. They can help traders identify potential entry and exit points. d1) ____________________ and d2) ____________________ are terms used to describe market conditions where the price of an asset has risen or fallen too far and is due for a correction. e) ____________________ is the process of identifying, assessing, and controlling risks that could negatively impact your trading strategy. f) ____________________ is a term used to describe a situation where the price of an asset is moving in the opposite direction of a technical indicator. g1) ____________________ and g2) ____________________ are levels on a price chart where the price of an asset has historically had difficulty breaking through. ____________________ h) are lines drawn on a price chart that connect two or more price points. They can help traders identify the direction of a trend. i) ____________________ is a measure of how much the price of an asset fluctuates over time. j) ____________________ is a measure of how much of an asset is being traded over a given period of time.

*See Solution on p. 199*

# Missing Vowel #7

## Learn about Technical Analysis

| Puzzle | Clue |
|---|---|
| _ N D _ C _ T _ R S | Tools that give directions on when to buy or sell a stock. |
| M _ V _ N G   _ V _ R _ G _ S | A filter that helps see the stock's trend more clearly. |
| C H _ R T   P _ T T _ R N S | Reading stock prices by its charts, to identify patterns that indicate a change in trend. |
| _ V _ R B _ _ G H T   _ N D   _ V _ R S _ L D | When a stock's price has risen or fallen too fast. |
| R _ S K   M _ N _ G _ M _ N T | Techniques to control and minimize potential losses and maximize potential gains of a trade. |
| D _ V _ R G _ N C _ | A difference between stock's price and an indicator that signals a change in trend. |
| S _ P P _ R T   _ N D   R _ S _ S T _ N C _ | Limits on how high or low a stock's price can go. |
| T R _ N D   L _ N _ S | Connecting price points to show the stock's current trend. |
| V _ L _ T _ L _ T Y | Measure of ups and downs in a stock's price. |
| V _ L _ M _ | Indicator of market sentiment towards a stock. |

*See Solution on p. 199*

# Double Puzzle #7

## A list of words that describe concepts of Technical Analysis

KRIS MNAEEMAGNT — 8 2 _ 39 / 36 37 106 _ 107 _ 29 7 116 24

IRIAONDTCS — 54 4 55 20 85 86 19 99 100 73

MNOVIG AEEAVRGS — 104 21 _ 51 62 _ / _ _ 66 _ 75 _ 12 _

SPOPRUT NDA RSANCIESTE — 47 10 _ _ _ 133 79 / 68 72 121 / _ 5 96 56 11 57 115 _ 60 80

RNDET SNELI — 102 122 132 127 77 / 50 28 76 40 94

HRCTA PETARNTS — 124 33 15 _ _ / _ 18 32 69 118 67 22 113

DGECVNREIE — _ 64 6 30 38 _ 126 90 81 34

VATILTOILY — 14 61 87 89 41 70 117 44 114 58

VMUOLE — _ _ 16 46 128 _

OEGBOVRHUT NDA OSOELVRD — 25 _ 48 _ _ _ 17 _ 82 27 / 91 83 _ / _ _ _ _ _ 63 71 92 65

1 ["] 2 / 4 5 6 7 8 / 10 11 12 / 14 15 16 17 18 19 20 21 22 / 24 25 / 27 28 29 30 / 32 33 34

36 37 38 39 40 41 42 [.] / 44 / 46 47 48 / 50 51 52 [Q] 53 [U] 54 55 56 57 58

60 61 62 63 64 65 66 67 68 69 70 71 72 73 / 75 76 77 / 79 80 81 82 83 84 [I] 85 86 87

89 90 91 92 93 [Y] 94 95 [I] 96 / 98 [F] 99 100 / 102 103 [I] 104 105 [I] 106 107 108 [.] 109 ["] / 111 [-] / 113 114 115 116 117 118 119 [Y]

121 122 123 [U] 124 125 [K] 126 127 128 129 [I] 130 [L] 131 [L] 132 133

*See Solution on p. 199*

## Cryptogram #7 - The Value of Technical Analysis

| A | B | C | D | E | F | G | H | I | J | K | L | M | N | O | P | Q | R | S | T | U | V | W | X | Y | Z |
|---|---|---|---|---|---|---|---|---|---|---|---|---|---|---|---|---|---|---|---|---|---|---|---|---|---|
| | | | | | | | | | | | | | | | | | | | | | | | | | |

X S E M    B F M E T H M M    E M    T Q X    R B Q F X

E T A H M X E T L    E T    L Y H R X

Z Q G V R T E H M    E X M    R B Q F X

V Y Q J E X E T L    J Y Q G    E T H J J E Z E H T X N O

V Y E Z H C    M X Q Z D M

- Michael Lauer

Why don't stock traders play cards in the jungle? Because there's too many cheetahs!

*See Solution on p. 199*

# Related Words Matching #7

### Associate Concepts of Technical Analysis to their Related Words:

| | | | |
|---|---|---|---|
| 1 | Support and resistance | A | liquidity, turnover, capacity, quantity, amount |
| 2 | Divergence | B | standard deviation, market fluctuations, black swan, flash crash, market correction |
| 3 | Moving averages | C | positive, negative, hidden, regular, bullish |
| 4 | Risk management | D | exponential, simple, weighted, hull, triangular |
| 5 | Volume | E | support, resistance, breakout, channel, wedge |
| 6 | Trend lines | F | head and shoulders, double top, double bottom, cup and handle, flag |
| 7 | Overbought and oversold | G | relative strength index (RSI), moving average convergence divergence (MACD), Bollinger bands, stochastic oscillator, average directional index |
| 8 | Chart patterns | H | overextended, overpriced, overvalued, undervalued, underpriced, underdone |
| 9 | Indicators | I | stop loss, position sizing, risk/reward ratio, trailing stop, maximum drawdown |
| 10 | Volatility | J | floor, foundation, base, underpinning, pillar |

*See Solution on p. 200*

# Multiple-Choice Quiz #7: Concepts of Technical Analysis

## Technical Analysis Analogies

- **Jim**: Hey Helen, I'm trying to wrap my head around some technical analysis terms. Can you help me out?
- **Helen**: Of course, Jim! What do you need help with?
- **Jim**: I'm not sure that I understand what risk management is.
- **Helen**: Think of it like a seatbelt for your investments. It's a way to protect yourself from potential losses by setting limits on how much you're willing to risk.
- **Jim**: Ah, I see. What about indicators?
- **Helen**: Indicators are like the dashboard of your car. They give you information about what's going on with a stock or other investment.
- **Jim:** Okay, I think I get it. How about moving averages?
- **Helen**: Moving averages are like a weather forecast. They give you an idea of what's likely to happen in the future based on what's happened in the past.
- **Jim**: Interesting. What about support and resistance?
- **Helen**: Support and resistance are like the floor and ceiling of a room. The floor is the support, and the ceiling is the resistance. Support and resistance levels are price points where a stock is likely to either bounce back up or fall back down.
- **Jim**: Got it. How about trend lines?
- **Helen**: Trend lines are like a map of a city. They help you see where the stock is headed and how fast it's moving.
- **Jim**: Okay, that makes sense. What about chart patterns?
- **Helen**: Chart patterns are like fingerprints. They're unique to each stock and can help you identify trends and predict future movements.
- **Jim**: I see. What about divergence?
- **Helen**: Divergence is like a fork in the road. It's a point where the stock is likely to either continue on its current path or change direction.
- **Jim**: Interesting. How about volatility?
- **Helen**: Volatility is like a rollercoaster. It's a measure of how much a stock's price is likely to change over time.
- **Jim**: I see. What about volume?
- **Helen**: Volume is like the number of people in a room. It's a measure of how many shares of a stock are being traded.
- **Jim:** Okay, I think I get it. What about overbought and oversold?
- **Helen**: Overbought and oversold are like a crowded elevator. When a stock is overbought, it's like the elevator is too full, and there's no more room for buyers. When a stock is oversold, it's like the elevator is empty, and there are no more sellers. In both cases, the stock is likely to change direction.
- **Jim**: Thanks, Helen! That was really helpful.

# Multiple-Choice Quiz #7: Concepts of Technical Analysis

| | |
|---|---|
| 1. **What is the analogy used to describe risk management?**<br>a) A city map<br>b) A seatbelt for investments<br>c) A crowded elevator<br>d) A weather forecast | 2. **How are indicators compared to other everyday items?**<br>a) Fingerprints<br>b) Moving averages<br>c) Support and resistance<br>d) A dashboard of a car |
| 3. **How are moving averages likened to something familiar?**<br>a) A seatbelt for investments<br>b) A weather forecast<br>c) A map of a city<br>d) The floor and ceiling of a room | 4. **In the analogy of support and resistance, what is compared to the floor and ceiling of a room?**<br>a) Moving averages<br>b) Volume<br>c) Divergence<br>d) Price points |
| 5. **How are trend lines described in the given analogy?**<br>a) Like fingerprints<br>b) Like a crowded elevator<br>c) Like a map of a city<br>d) Like the number of people in a room | 6. **What is the analogy used to describe chart patterns?**<br>a) A seatbelt for investments<br>b) Fingerprints<br>c) Unique to each stock<br>d) A weather forecast |
| 7. **How is divergence compared to something familiar?**<br>a) A crowded elevator<br>b) A fork in the road<br>c) A weather forecast<br>d) The number of people in a room | 8. **What is the analogy used to describe volatility?**<br>a) A rollercoaster<br>b) A crowded elevator<br>c) A seatbelt for investments<br>d) A fork in the road |
| 9. **In the given analogy, what is volume compared to?**<br>a) A city map<br>b) A weather forecast<br>c) The number of people in a room<br>d) A seatbelt for investments | 10- **How are overbought and oversold described in the analogy?**<br>a) Like fingerprints<br>b) Like a crowded elevator<br>c) Like a map of a city<br>d) Like a seatbelt for investments |

*See Solution on p. 200*

# Unit 8: Stock Market Idioms

An idiom is a phrase or expression whose meaning is not predictable from the usual meanings of its individual words. Idioms often carry a figurative meaning that is understood by a particular group of people or within a specific cultural context. They can add color, depth, and nuance to language, but their interpretation may not be straightforward for those who are not familiar with the idiomatic usage.

For example, the idiom "to cook the books" means to manipulate or falsify financial records, typically for fraudulent or deceptive purposes. When someone is accused of cooking the books, it implies that they are altering accounting records, inflating or deflating financial figures, or engaging in other dishonest practices to misrepresent the true financial health of a business or organization. This can be done for various reasons, such as to deceive investors, creditors, or regulatory authorities. In essence, "cooking the books" involves unethical and illegal actions related to financial reporting.

# Unit 8: Stock Market Idioms

Mastering stock market idioms can be a practical and valuable skill to help you enhance your language proficiency and facilitate your success in professional and academic contexts.

Here's a list of ten more stock market idioms:

1. **Bear hug**: A strategy where an investor or company aggressively and persistently pursues another to acquire it.
2. **Black swan**: An unexpected and rare event that has a major impact on the financial markets.
3. **Cut one's losses**: Selling investments to minimize losses before they become more significant.
4. **FOMO** (Fear of Missing Out): The anxiety or apprehension about missing out on a profitable investment opportunity.
5. **Fool's gold**: Investments that seem valuable but turn out to be worthless or not as profitable as expected.
6. **To hedge your bets**: Taking actions to reduce the risk of losing money by making additional investments or protective measures.
7. **To the moon**: Refers to the expectation or desire for a stock's price to increase significantly.

# Unit 8: Stock Market Idioms

8. **To ride the bull**: Taking advantage of a strong and rising market trend for financial gain.
9. **Play the market**: Engaging in buying, selling, or trading financial instruments with the aim of making a profit.
10. **Sitting on your cash**: Holding onto cash instead of investing it, often in anticipation of better opportunities.

## Word Search Puzzle #8 - Stock Market Idioms
## Find Stock Market Common Idioms in the list below:

| | | | | | | | | | | | | | | | |
|---|---|---|---|---|---|---|---|---|---|---|---|---|---|---|---|
| S | T | E | B | R | U | O | Y | E | G | D | E | H | N | H | J |
| P | S | Z | J | M | R | I | D | E | T | H | E | B | U | L | L |
| X | E | Q | Z | O | W | W | M | P | D | J | F | D | J | I | O |
| W | S | X | E | D | L | O | G | S | L | O | O | F | X | P | J |
| M | S | V | T | X | B | B | J | N | A | M | M | C | P | D | U |
| S | O | Z | O | J | L | D | A | B | Y | J | W | K | I | Y | B |
| P | L | T | T | T | A | O | W | B | L | C | V | F | E | V | T |
| F | S | E | H | H | C | W | X | A | K | I | B | T | G | B | J |
| N | E | B | E | G | K | L | H | S | G | N | E | J | X | G | Z |
| N | N | M | M | W | S | T | K | N | S | F | A | X | W | Y | S |
| V | O | D | O | S | W | G | W | T | C | G | R | J | T | Z | I |
| E | T | K | O | U | A | D | A | V | W | X | H | P | R | K | G |
| S | U | Q | N | O | N | H | F | O | M | O | U | T | A | U | B |
| Z | C | B | R | P | X | U | S | B | V | P | G | B | K | V | J |
| P | L | A | Y | T | H | E | M | A | R | K | E | T | C | O | H |
| Z | R | J | X | W | T | I | Z | E | D | A | I | C | G | R | F |

BEAR HUG
CUT ONE'S LOSSES
FOOL'S GOLD
PLAY THE MARKET
TO THE MOON

BLACK SWAN
FOMO
HEDGE YOUR BETS
RIDE THE BULL

*See Solution on p. 200*

# Crossword Puzzle #8

## Learn about Stock Market Idioms

Across

**[1]** Expectation of significant price increase in a stock.

**[3]** Take advantage of a rising market by holding onto or buying stocks.

**[5]** Minimize risk by diversifying investments.

**[6]** Holding onto cash rather than investing it.

**[8]** Engage in buying and selling securities to make a profit.

**[10]** Investment that appears valuable but is ultimately worthless.

Down

**[2]** Aggressive and friendly takeover attempt.

**[4]** Fear of Missing Out.

**[7]** Sell investments to minimize losses before they increase.

**[9]** Unpredictable and rare market event with severe consequences.

*See Solution on p. 200*

## Scramble Puzzle #8 - Stock Market Idioms

**Uncramble the different stock market idioms in the list below**

FO'OLS LGDO

TCU 'EOSN LSESOS

OT ETH OMNO

AREB UGH

EEGHD UYRO ETSB

YPLA ETH MKERAT

RAFE FO MSNIISG TOU

STTINIG NO OURY SCHA

IERD HET LLUB

LKCBA ANWS

*See Solution on p. 201*

# Definition Match-Up #8

Stock Mark Idioms

## Associate the *Idioms* to their Definition

| | | | |
|---|---|---|---|
| **1** | FOMO | **A** | A strategy where an investor or company aggressively and persistently pursues another to acquire it. |
| **2** | Play the market | **B** | Selling investments to minimize losses before they become more significant. |
| **3** | To the moon | **C** | An unexpected and rare event that has a major impact on the financial markets. |
| **4** | Hedge your bets | **D** | Taking advantage of a strong and rising market trend for financial gain. |
| **5** | Bear hug | **E** | The anxiety or apprehension about missing out on a profitable investment opportunity. |
| **6** | Fool's gold | **F** | Holding onto cash instead of investing it, often in anticipation of better opportunities. |
| **7** | Cut one's losses | **G** | Investments that seem valuable but turn out to be worthless or not as profitable as expected. |
| **8** | Black swan | **H** | Taking actions to reduce the risk of losing money by making additional investments or protective measures. |
| **9** | Sitting on your cash | **I** | Engaging in buying, selling, or trading financial instruments with the aim of making a profit. |
| **10** | Ride the bull | **J** | Refers to the expectation or desire for a stock's price to increase significantly. |

*See Solution on p. 201*

# Cloze Test #8

## Fill In the Blanks Using the Idioms below:

Bear hug - Black swan - Cut one's losses - FOMO - Fool's gold - Hedge your bets - To the moon - Ride the bull - Play the market - Sitting on your cash

Explore the dynamic world of the stock market through the tale of friends Tim and Lisa.

Tim, a wise investor, believed in a) ____________ through diversification, cautioning Lisa about the allure of seemingly promising stocks, akin to b) ____________.

Lisa sought Tim's advice to c) ____________ of market trends but was reminded to avoid d) ____________.

Tim shared a cautionary tale about e) ____________ and emphasized strategic timing instead of merely f) ____________.

Their talk turned to a unique investment approach – the g) ____________. Tim stressed the importance of being prepared for unexpected h) ____________ events.

As the sun set, Tim pointed to the sky, mentioning the market soaring i) ____________. Success lies in staying informed, making prudent choices, relishing the journey, and sometimes, j) ____________ for the right opportunity.

*See Solution on p. 201*

# Missing Vowel #8

**Learn about Stock Market Idioms**

| Puzzle | Clue |
|---|---|
| R _ D _   T H _   B _ L L | Taking advantage of rising market trends, expecting prices to go up. |
| H _ D G _   Y _ _ R   B _ T S | Diversifying investments to reduce risk by spreading assets. |
| C _ T   _ N _ ' S   L _ S S _ S | Selling investments early to minimize losses. |
| F _ _ L ' S   G _ L D | Investments that seem valuable but turn out to be worth much less. |
| S _ T T _ N G   _ N   Y _ _ R   C _ S H | Holding onto cash, waiting for the right opportunity to invest. |
| F _ M _ | Anxiety about missing profitable opportunities. |
| B L _ C K   S W _ N | Unexpected and rare events with a significant impact on markets. |
| P L _ Y   T H _   M _ R K _ T | Engaging in buying, selling, or trading for profit. |
| T _   T H _   M _ _ N | Expecting a significant increase in a stock's price. |
| B _ _ R   H _ G | An aggressive strategy of persistently pursuing another company for acquisition. |

*See Solution on p. 201*

# Double Puzzle #8

## A list of idioms related to the stock market

| Scrambled | Numbered letters |
|---|---|
| EDRI ETH LBUL | 7 53 10 / 58 51 |
| GDHEE OURY ETSB | 9 49 / 12 |
| TCU 'ESNO LSOESS | 29 59 23 52 42 |
| FO'OLS OLDG | 20 30 11 8 60 |
| SNITTIG NO UYRO HCAS | 16 26 31 15 37 38 57 54 40 14 34 56 |
| MFOO | 19 48 |
| KACBL ASNW | 6 50 17 27 22 41 |
| YAPL HET MEKART | 24 4 35 2 |
| OT HET NOMO | 33 3 61 |
| ABRE GHU | |

" _ _ _ (1 2 3 4) _ _ _ _ _ _ _ (6 7 8 9 10 11 12) _ _ _ _ (14 15 16 17) _ _ (19 20) _ _ _ (22 23 24) _ _ (26 27) _ _ _ (29 30 31)

_ _ _ I _ _ (33 34 35 36 37 38) _ _ _ . " (40 41 42 43 44) — (46) _ _ _ _ _ _ _ (48 49 50 51 52 53 54) _ _ _ _ _ _ (56 57 58 59 60 61)

*See Solution on p. 202*

# Cryptogram #8 - Stock Market Idioms

| A | B | C | D | E | F | G | H | I | J | K | L | M | N | O | P | Q | R | S | T | U | V | W | X | Y | Z |
|---|---|---|---|---|---|---|---|---|---|---|---|---|---|---|---|---|---|---|---|---|---|---|---|---|---|
| | | | | | | | | | | | | | | | | | | | | | | | | | |

FPIF LMN NPIF JA L

QELPNPSGMR ATWGIG JM RWG

ARBTH ILEHGR ZWGEG RWG

FEJTG BQ L ARBTH JA

LERJQJTJLSSD JMQSLRGN LMN

RWGM RWG ATWGIGEA AGSS BQQ

RWGJE AWLEGA SGLXJMV BRWGE

JMXGARBEA ZJRW SBAAGA

- Anonymous

*See Solution on p. 202*

# Related Words Matching #8

## Associate the Stock Market Idioms to their Related Words:

| | | | |
|---|---|---|---|
| 1 | FOMO | A | aggressive takeover, hostile acquisition, intense business embrace, acquisition strongly pursued strategic business grasp |
| 2 | Play the market | B | unpredictable event, rare and unforeseen occurrence, unexpected financial event, unprecedented market shift, rare and impactful incident |
| 3 | To the moon | C | trade strategically, participate in trading, engage in market moves, speculate on investments, navigate financial waters |
| 4 | Hedge your bets | D | deceptive investment, illusory profit, misleading opportunity, false wealth, shiny but worthless |
| 5 | Bear hug | E | cut loss, exit prudently, save investments, financial retreat, tactical withdrawal |
| 6 | Fool's gold | F | capitalize on market optimism, benefit from positive trends, bullish participation, handle rising prices, gain from market upswing |
| 7 | Cut one's losses | G | skyrocketing prices, exponential growth, astronomical returns, soaring high, to infinity and beyond |
| 8 | Black swan | H | investment anxiety, missing the boat, greed influence, herd mentality |
| 9 | Sitting on your cash | I | diversify investments, spread risk, ensure safety net, balance portfolio, risk management |
| 10 | Ride the bull | J | holding liquid assets, awaiting opportunities, cash reserve, waiting for the right moment, financial patience |

*See Solution on p. 202*

# Multiple-Choice Quiz #8: Stock Market Idioms

## Stock Market Idioms

- **Ted:** Hey Sue, have you been following the stock market lately?

- **Sue:** Yeah, I've been trying to figure it out. It's like a whole different language sometimes.

- **Ted**: True! You know, it's always good to diversify your investments, kind of like hedging your bets.

- **Sue**: Diversify? Isn't that like not putting all your eggs in one basket?

- **Ted**: Exactly! You don't want to risk everything on one thing. Speaking of risk, did you hear about Dave investing in that new tech startup?

- **Sue**: No, what happened?

- **Ted**: Well, it's a bit like fool's gold. He thought it was a sure thing, but turns out, not so much.

- **Sue**: Yikes! That's why I'm cautious about jumping into investments. I don't want to get caught up in the FOMO and regret it later.

- **Ted**: Smart move. You've got to be careful not to chase after trends blindly. By the way, are you still holding onto that extra cash?

- **Sue**: Yeah, I've been sitting on my cash for a while now. Waiting for the right opportunity.

- **Ted**: Well, timing is everything. Sometimes you've got to cut your losses and move on.

- **Sue**: True. Have you noticed how some companies try to acquire others aggressively?

- **Ted**: Yeah, it's like a big, tight hug – a bear hug. Happens a lot in the business world.

- **Sue**: Interesting. And what about those who always seem to predict the market will go to the moon?

- **Ted**: Ah, the eternal optimists! They believe stocks will soar high. It's like they're always ready to ride the bull.

- **Sue**: So, you think they're just playing the market?

- **Ted**: Exactly. It's a game, and everyone's got their strategy.

# Multiple-Choice Quiz #8: Stock Market Idioms

| | |
|---|---|
| 1. **What does Ted mean by "hedging your bets" in the dialogue??**<br>a) Taking advantage of a rising market trend<br>b) Diversifying investments to reduce risk<br>c) Making quick and risky investments<br>d) Betting on a specific stock | 2. **How does Sue interpret the idea of diversification in investing?**<br>a) Spreading assets across various options<br>b) Concentrating all investments in one basket<br>c) Investing only in tech startups<br>d) Avoiding investments altogether |
| 3. **In the dialogue, what does Ted compare the new tech startup investment to?**<br>a) Fool's gold<br>b) FOMO<br>c) To the moon<br>d) Bear hug | 4. **What is Sue cautious about, expressing a fear of regret later?**<br>a) Black swan events<br>b) Riding the bull<br>c) Fool's gold<br>d) FOMO |
| 5. **What does Sue mean by "sitting on her cash"?**<br>a) Holding onto cash, waiting for the right opportunity<br>b) Making quick and impulsive investments<br>c) Selling all her investments<br>d) Investing in diverse portfolios | 6. **What does Ted suggest about timing in investments?**<br>a) Timing doesn't matter in investing<br>b) Timing is essential, and sometimes you have to cut your losses<br>c) Timing is irrelevant when playing the market<br>d) Timing is only crucial in bear hug situations |
| 7. **In the dialogue, what analogy does Ted use to describe aggressive acquisitions in the business world?**<br>a) Riding the bull<br>b) To the moon<br>c) Bear hug<br>d) Playing the market | 8. **What does Sue ask about individuals who predict the market will "go to the moon"?**<br>a) Are they sitting on their cash?<br>b) Do they play the market?<br>c) Do they believe in black swan events?<br>d) Are they chasing trends blindly? |
| 9. **How does Ted describe those who predict the market will "go to the moon"?**<br>a) Sitting on their cash<br>b) Playing the market<br>c) Riding the bull<br>d) FOMO enthusiasts | 10- **According to Ted in the dialogue, what is investing in the stock market compared to?**<br>a) A game with various strategies<br>b) A risky and impulsive decision<br>c) A fool's gold opportunity<br>d) A bear hug situation |

*See Solution on p. 202*

# Conclusion

Bravo on completing your adventure through the stock market! By delving into the world of finance and understanding its terminology, you've equipped yourself with valuable knowledge that will undoubtedly benefit you in various aspects of your life.

Throughout this book, you've explored the intricacies of the stock market, from its fundamental concepts to its practical applications. You've learned about the different sectors of the economy, the participants involved, various trading instruments, and strategies used by investors. You've also delved into the realms of technical and fundamental analysis, gaining insights into how to assess market trends and analyze company performance.

Beyond the financial knowledge, you've also enhanced your English language skills. The engaging exercises and vocabulary-building activities have helped you master the terminology necessary for effective communication in business and financial contexts. This newfound linguistic proficiency will undoubtedly boost your confidence and open doors to new opportunities.

As you move forward, remember that the stock market is a dynamic and ever-evolving field. It's essential to stay updated with the latest trends, news, and developments. By continuing to learn and explore, you'll be well-positioned to make informed decisions and successfully make your way through the complexities of the financial world.

Thank you for choosing this book as your guide. We hope it has been a valuable resource in your learning journey. Good luck!

# Answer Keys

## A.K. of Quiz #1 p. 7

### SOLUTION

1. c
2. a
3. d
4. b
5. c

## A.K. of Word Search #1 p. 12

Word Search Puzzle #1 - The 11 Sectors of the Economy - Solution

| C | | | M | | | | | | | | | | | | |
|---|---|---|---|---|---|---|---|---|---|---|---|---|---|---|---|
| O | | D | A | | T | | | | | | | | | | S |
| N | | I | T | H | E | | | | | | | | | E | R |
| S | | S | E | E | C | | | | | | | | L | | E |
| U | I | C | R | A | H | | | | | | | P | U | | A |
| M | N | R | I | L | N | C | | | | | A | | T | | L |
| E | D | E | A | T | O | O | | | | T | | | I | | E |
| R | U | T | L | H | L | N | | | S | | | | L | | S |
| S | S | I | S | C | O | S | | R | | | | | I | | T |
| E | T | O | | A | G | U | E | | | | Y | | T | | A |
| R | R | N | | R | Y | M | | | | G | | | I | | T |
| V | I | A | | E | U | E | | | R | | | | E | | E |
| I | A | R | | S | | R | | E | | | | | S | | |
| C | L | Y | N | | F | I | N | A | N | C | I | A | L | S | |
| E | S | O | | | | E | | | | | | | | | |
| S | C | | | | | | | | | | | | | | |

## A.K. Crossword #1 p. 13

### SOLUTION

[1→] Discretionary
[2↓] Services
[3↓] Staples
[4↓] Energy
[5→] Financials
[6↓] Healthcare
[7↓] Industrials
[8→] Materials
[9→] Real Estate
[10↓] Technology
[11→] Utilities

## A.K. Scramble Puzzle #1 p. 14

Scramble Puzzle #1 - The 11 Sectors of the Economy - Solution

Unscramble the 11 sectors of the economy words in the list below

| | |
|---|---|
| CESMNOUR DRTESRNIAOICY | CONSUMER DISCRETIONARY |
| CSEUNOMR SLTAEPS | CONSUMER STAPLES |
| TCOELOGNHY | TECHNOLOGY |
| HAEHCRALTE | HEALTHCARE |
| MTRALAIES | MATERIALS |
| IASRUDLNTIS | INDUSTRIALS |
| ERGENY | ENERGY |
| UEIITTLIS | UTILITIES |
| ALER EASTTE | REAL ESTATE |
| CEOUMNSR SRIECEVS | CONSUMER SERVICES |

## A.K. Definition Match-Up #1 p. 15

**SOLUTION**

1- Healthcare = F
2- Materials = H
3- Real Estate = I
4- Consumer Staples = C
5- Consumer Discretionary = A
6- Utilities = K
7- Energy = D
8- Industrials = G
9- Consumer Services = B
10- Financials = E
11- Technology = J

## A.K. of Cloze Test #1 p. 16

### Cloze Test #1

**Fill In the Banks Using the 11 Sectors of the Economy**

SOLUTION

1. **Healthcare** is a vital industry that provides essential clinical services to people around the world.
2. **Materials** are the raw ingredients that are used to create a wide variety of products, from buildings to consumer goods.
3. **Real Estate** involves the buying, selling, and management of properties such as homes, offices, and retail spaces.
4. **Consumer Staples** are everyday items that people need to live, such as food, clothing, and personal care products.
5. **Consumer Discretionary** refers to products and services that people can choose to buy, such as electronics, vacations, and luxury goods.
6. **Utilities** provide essential services like electricity, gas, and water to households and businesses.
7. **Energy** refers to the production, distribution, and use of power, including fossil fuels and renewable sources.
8. **Industrials** include a wide range of businesses, from manufacturing to transportation.
9. **Consumer Services** include industries such as retail, tourism, and entertainment.
10. **Financials** encompass banks, insurance companies, and investment firms.
11. **Technology** encompasses the development and use of computer systems, software, and networks.

## A.K. Missing Vowel #1 p. 17

### Missing Vowel #1 - Solution

Learn about the 11 Sectors of the Stock Market

| | |
|---|---|
| CONSUMER SERVICES | About services such as education and healthcare. |
| UTILITIES | About services such as water and electricity. |
| CONSUMER DISCRETIONARY | About luxury goods and recreation. |
| FINANCIALS | About money-related services such as banks and insurance. |
| HEALTHCARE | About health-related products and services. |
| TECHNOLOGY | About IT products and services. |
| ENERGY | About energy production and distribution. |
| MATERIALS | About raw materials such as chemicals and metals. |
| REAL ESTATE | About property ownership and management. |
| INDUSTRIALS | About manufacturing, construction, and transportation-related goods and services. |

## A.K. Double Puzzle #1 p. 18

### Double Puzzle #1 - Solution

A list of words that describe the 11 sectors of the economy

| | |
|---|---|
| HLACHEARTE | HEALTHCARE |
| MRLTAEIAS | MATERIALS |
| ELRA EATTSE | REAL ESTATE |
| CEUNOSMR SLEAPTS | CONSUMER STAPLES |
| CSMEOUNR DNEIIASCRTROY | CONSUMER DISCRETIONARY |
| UTIILETIS | UTILITIES |
| EEGNRY | ENERGY |
| ILTRUSANIDS | INDUSTRIALS |
| CUSMNEOR SECIREVS | CONSUMER SERVICES |
| FCINAINLAS | FINANCIALS |
| TNHOLCOGEY | TECHNOLOGY |

THE STOCK MARKET

## A.K. Cryptogram #1 p. 19

I WILL TELL YOU HOW TO BECOME RICH. CLOSE THE DOORS. BE FEARFUL WHEN OTHERS ARE GREEDY. BE GREEDY WHEN OTHERS ARE FEARFUL. - Warren Buffett

## A.K. Related Words Matching #1 p. 20

Related Words Matching #1

Solution

Associate the Sectors of the Economy to their Family of Words:

| # | Sector | Letter | Family of Words |
|---|---|---|---|
| 1 | Consumer Discretionary | I | luxury goods, leisure, entertainment, fashion, retail |
| 2 | Consumer Services | D | retail, hospitality, restaurants, travel, entertainment |
| 3 | Consumer Staples | G | food, beverages, household goods, groceries, toiletries |
| 4 | Energy | F | oil, gas, renewable energy, fossil fuels, electricity |
| 5 | Financials | J | banking, insurance, investment, finance, stocks |
| 6 | Healthcare | E | medicine, treatment, hospitals, clinics, pharmaceuticals |
| 7 | Industrials | K | manufacturing, construction, machinery, transportation, engineering |
| 8 | Materials | C | raw materials, metals, minerals, chemicals, plastics |
| 9 | Real Estate | H | property, housing, land, commercial, residential |
| 10 | Technology | A | software, hardware, computers, electronics, internet |
| 11 | Utilities | B | electricity, gas, water, sanitation, telecommunications |

## A.K. Multiple-Choice Puzzle #1 p. 22

**SOLUTION**

1. D
2. D
3. A
4. D
5. D
6. C
7. A
8. B
9. B
10. D

## A.K. of Word Search # 2 p. 25

Word Search Puzzle #2 - The 7 Participants in the Stock Market

Find the 7 participants of the stock market in the list below:

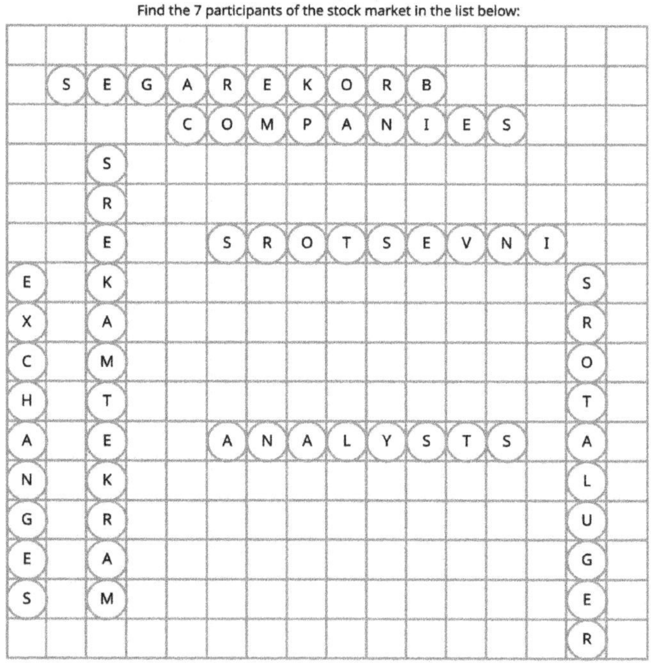

| A.K. of Crossword Puzzle #2 p. 26 | A.K. Scramble Puzzle #2 p. 27 |
|---|---|

## Crossword Puzzle #2

Learn about the 7 Participants in the Stock Market

[1↓] Companies
[2→] Investors
[3↓] Brokerages
[4→] Exchanges
[5↓] Regulators
[6→] Market Makers
[7→] Analysts

### Scramble #2 - The 7 Participants in the Stock Market - Solution

**Uncramble the words in the list below:**

| | |
|---|---|
| CPIMOENAS | C O M P A N I E S |
| IESVORTNS | I N V E S T O R S |
| BOAGRKEERS | B R O K E R A G E S |
| EEXANCHGS | E X C H A N G E S |
| ROALTEGRUS | R E G U L A T O R S |
| MKERAT MRAKES | M A R K E T M A K E R S |
| ATLYNASS | A N A L Y S T S |

| A.K. Definition Match-Up #2 p. 28 | A.K. Cloze Test #2 p. 29 |
|---|---|

## Definition Match-Up #2

The 7 Participants in the Stock Market

**Associate the 7 Participants in the Stock Market to their Definitions: SOLUTION**

| | | | |
|---|---|---|---|
| 1 | Companies | A | Legal entities that engage in business activities. Can be publicly traded (must disclose certain financial info) or privately held. |
| 2 | Investors | B | Buy securities with the expectation of earning a return. May seek income or capital appreciation. |
| 3 | Brokerages | C | Financial firms that help clients buy and sell securities. Can be full-service or discount. |
| 4 | Exchanges | D | Marketplaces where securities are bought and sold. Examples include NYSE, NASDAQ, and TSE. |
| 5 | Regulators | E | Agencies or organizations that oversee and regulate financial markets. Examples include SEC and FCA. |
| 6 | Market makers | F | Financial institutions or individuals that stand ready to buy or sell securities at any time, providing liquidity to markets. |
| 7 | Analysts | G | Professionals who study and evaluate financial and economic data to make recommendations to investors. May work for brokerages, investment banks, or other financial institutions and may specialize in certain industries or sectors. |

## Cloze Test #2

**Fill In the Banks Using the 7 Participants in the Stock market**

a) investors - b) analysts - c) Brokerages - d) Exchanges - e) Regulators - f)Market makers - g) Companies

**SOLUTION**

**g) Companies** listed on **d) exchanges** around the world rely on a variety of different players to help them achieve success in the financial markets. Shareholders, for example, provide the capital that companies need to fund their operations and grow their businesses. Without the support of financiers, many companies would struggle to survive. **c) Brokerages**, on the other hand, facilitate the buying and selling of stocks on behalf of their clients, helping to ensure that there is always liquidity in the market. Marketplaces, such as the New York Stock Exchange and the NASDAQ, provide the platforms on which stocks are traded and listed. **e) Regulators**, including the Securities and Exchange Commission (SEC) in the United States, are responsible for overseeing and regulating the financial markets to ensure that they operate fairly and transparently. **f) Market makers**, who are usually large financial institutions, also play a crucial role in the financial markets by providing liquidity and helping to match buyers and sellers. Finally, **b) analysts**, who may be employed by trading firms or other financial firms, provide research and recommendations to help **a) investors** make informed decisions about which stocks to buy or sell. Overall, the interactions between these various players help to create a healthy and functioning financial market.

| # A.K. of Missing Vowel #2 p. 30 | # A.K. Double Puzzle #2 p. 31 |
|---|---|

## Missing Vowel #2 - Solution

**Learn about the 7 participants in the Stock Market**

| | |
|---|---|
| E X C H A N G E S | platforms where stocks and other securities are traded and listed |
| M A R K E T M A K E R S | they facilitate the buying and selling of securities by providing liquidity to the market |
| R E G U L A T O R S | they oversee and regulate financial markets to ensure fair and transparent operations |
| C O M P A N I E S | they issue stocks and are listed on exchanges |
| I N V E S T O R S | they buy and sell stocks |
| B R O K E R A G E S | they facilitate the buying and selling of stocks on behalf of clients |
| A N A L Y S T S | they study and provide research on stocks and other securities |

## Double Puzzle #2 - Solution

**A list of words that describe the 7 Participants in the Stock Market**

| | |
|---|---|
| ALSYATNS | A N A L Y S T S (69 17 65 87 7 24) |
| IROVENTSS | I N V E S T O R S (9 40 6 1 13 64) |
| CNIEPMAOS | C O M P A N I E S (32 83 75 68 59 60 16 42 10) |
| BOEEARKRGS | B R O K E R A G E S (27 30 5 23 14 54 18 48) |
| MREAKT MREAKS | M A R K E T M A K E R S (76 33 78 37 29 39 15 71 77 67) |
| EANGCEXHS | E X C H A N G E S (3 46 2 35 49 34) |
| RTOGELURAS | R E G U L A T O R S (56 26 22 88 86 20 21 70) |

THE KEY IS WORKING TOGETHER TO CREATE AN EFFICIENT, FAIR, AND TRANSPARENT MARKET FOR ALL.

# A.K. Cryptogram #2 p. 32

1. BROKERAGES AND DEALERS USE SPECIALIZED SOFTWARE AND ALGORITHMS TO EXECUTE TRADES AT LIGHTNING SPEEDS, SOMETIMES COMPLETING A TRADE IN LESS THAN A MILLISECOND.

# A.K. of Related Words #2 p. 33

## Related Words Matching #2

**Associate the Sectors of the Economy to their Family of Words:**

SOLUTION

| | | | |
|---|---|---|---|
| 1 | Companies | A | business, corporation, firm, enterprise, organization |
| 2 | Investors | B | shareholders, stockholders, creditors, financiers, backers |
| 3 | Brokerages | C | firms, houses, agencies, dealerships, bureaus |
| 4 | Exchanges | D | markets, platforms, bourses, venues, boards |
| 5 | Regulators | E | authorities, overseers, controllers, monitors, supervisors |
| 6 | Market makers | F | dealers, brokers, liquidity providers, underwriters, jobbers |
| 7 | Analysts | G | researchers, experts, commentators, consultants, advisers |

## A.K. of Multiple-Choice Quiz #2 p. 35

1- d. Companies
2- d. Investors
3- c. Brokerages
4- c. Market makers
5- c. Analysts
6- d. Regulators
7- c. Exchanges
8- b. Market makers
9- c. Exchanges
10- d. All of the above

## A.K. Word Search #3a p. 44

Word Search Puzzle #3a - Trading Instruments (securities and equities) - Solution

| | | | | | | | | | | | | | | | |
|---|---|---|---|---|---|---|---|---|---|---|---|---|---|---|---|
| | | | | C | U | R | R | E | N | C | I | E | S | | |
| | | C | O | M | M | O | D | I | T | I | E | S | | | |
| | | C | F | D | S | | | | | | | | | | |
| | | | | | | | | | | | | | | | |
| | | | | | | | | | O | | | | | | |
| S | | | | | S | F | T | E | | P | | | | | |
| | T | | | | | | | | | | T | | | | |
| | | O | | | S | E | R | U | T | U | F | I | | B | |
| | | | C | | | | | | | | | | O | | |
| | | | | K | | | | | | | | N | | N | |
| | | | | | S | | | | | | D | | | | S |
| | | | | | | | | | | S | | | | | |
| | | | | | | | | | | | | | | | |
| | | | | | | | | | | | | | | | |
| | | | | | | | | | | | | | | | |

## A.K. Word Search #3b p. 45

Word Search Puzzle #3b - Trading Instruments (securities and equities) - Solution

| | | | | | | | | | | | | | | C | S |
|---|---|---|---|---|---|---|---|---|---|---|---|---|---|---|---|
| | | | | | | S | | | | | | | | O | T |
| | | | | | K | | | | | | | | | N | N |
| | | | | C | | | | | | | | | | V | A |
| | | | O | | | | | | | | | | M | E | R |
| | | T | | | | | | | | | | S | U | R | R |
| | S | | | | F | | | | | | | N | T | T | A |
| | | | | | | U | | | | | | O | U | I | W |
| | | | | | | | T | | | | | I | A | B | |
| | | | | | | B | | U | | | | T | L | L | |
| | | | | | | E | O | | R | | | P | F | E | |
| | | | | | | T | | N | | E | | O | U | B | |
| | | | | | | F | | | D | | S | | N | O | |
| | | | | | | S | | | | S | | | D | N | |
| | | | | | | | | | | | | | S | D | |
| | | | | | | | | | | | | | | S | |

## A.K. Word Search #3c p. 46

Word Search Puzzle #3c - Trading Instruments (securities and equities) - Solution

| | | | | | | | | | | | | | | | |
|---|---|---|---|---|---|---|---|---|---|---|---|---|---|---|---|
| S | E | I | T | I | D | O | M | M | O | C | T | F | O | S | |
| | | | | | | | | | | | | | | | |
| | | | | | | | | | | | | | | | |
| | | | | | | | | | | | | | | | |
| | | F | O | R | E | S | T | P | R | O | D | U | C | T | S |
| | | A | G | R | I | C | U | L | T | U | R | E | | | |
| | | | | | | | | | | | | | | | |
| | | | | | | | | | M | | | | | E | |
| | | | | | | | | E | | | | | N | | |
| | | | | | | | T | | | | | E | | | |
| | | | | | | A | | | | | R | | | | |
| | | | | | L | | | | | G | | | | | |
| | | | | | | | | | Y | | | | | | |
| | | S | E | N | O | T | S | S | U | O | I | C | E | R | P |
| L | I | V | E | S | T | O | C | K | A | N | D | M | E | A | T |

**A.K. Word Search #3d p. 47**

Word Search Puzzle #3d - Trading Instruments (securities and equities) - Solution

| | | | | | | | | | | | | | | | |
|---|---|---|---|---|---|---|---|---|---|---|---|---|---|---|---|
| | | | | | | | | | | | S | | | P | D |
| | | | | | | | | | P | K | | G | R | V | E |
| | | | | | | | | I | C | | R | E | A | D | F |
| | | | | | | | H | O | | O | F | L | | I | E |
| | | | | | | C | T | | W | E | U | P | | V | N |
| | | | | | E | S | | T | R | E | | E | | I | S |
| | | | | U | N | | H | R | S | | | N | | D | I |
| | | | L | O | | S | E | T | | | | N | | E | V |
| | | B | M | | T | D | O | | | | | Y | | N | E |
| | | M | | O | S | C | | | | | | S | | D | S |
| | O | | C | T | K | | | | | | | T | | S | T |
| C | | K | O | S | | | | | | | | O | | T | O |
| | S | C | | | | | | | | | | C | | O | C |
| | K | | | | | | | | | | | K | | C | K |
| | | | | | | | | | | | | S | | K | S |
| | | | | | | | | | | | | | | S | |

**A.K. Crossword Puzzle #3a p. 48**

# Crossword Puzzle #3a

Learn about Trading Instruments

[1↓] Stocks
[2→] Options
[3→] Futures
[4↓] Etfs
[5→] Currencies
[6↓] Commodities
[7→] Bonds
[8↓] Cfds

**A.K. Crossword Puzzle #3b p. 49**

# Crossword Puzzle #3b

Learn about Types of Securities

[1→] Stocks
[2↓] Bonds
[3↓] Options
[4↓] Futures
[5→] Mutual Funds
[6↓] Etfs
[7↓] Warrants
[8→] Convertible Bonds

**A.K. Crossword Puzzle #3c p. 50**

# Crossword Puzzle #3c

Learn about Types of Commodities

[1↓] Agriculture
[2↓] Energy
[3↓] Metal
[4→] Livestock And Meat
[5→] Soft Commodities
[6↓] Forest Products
[7→] Precious Stones
[8→] Financial Commodities

| A.K. Crossword Puzzle #3d p.51 | A.K. Scramble Puzzle #3a p. 52 |
|---|---|

# Crossword Puzzle #3d

Learn about Types of Stocks

[1↓] Common Stocks
[2→] Preferred Stock
[3↓] Blue-Chip Stocks
[4↓] Penny Stocks
[5→] Growth Stocks
[6↓] Value Stocks
[7→] Dividend Stocks
[8→] Defensive Stocks

Scramble Puzzle #3a - Trading Instruments - Solution

Uncramble the Trading Instruments in the list below

CNREERIUCS C U R R E N C I E S
CEMOTIOMDIS C O M M O D I T I E S
ODSNB B O N D S
SKCTOS S T O C K S
FEST E T F S
OTINPOS O P T I O N S
SDCF C F D S
FTREUUS F U T U R E S

| A.K. Scramble Puzzle #3b p. 53 | A.K. Scramble Puzzle #3c p. 54 |
|---|---|

Scramble Puzzle #3b - Trading Instruments - Solution

Uncramble the Types of Securities in the list below

NBSOD B O N D S
CELITBRNVOE NSDOB C O N V E R T I B L E B O N D S
FEST E T F S
FTEUURS F U T U R E S
MAUTUL DSUNF M U T U A L F U N D S
ONPTIOS O P T I O N S
SCTKOS S T O C K S
WTNRAARS W A R R A N T S

Scramble Puzzle #3c - Trading Instruments - Solution

Uncramble the Types of Commodities in the list below

FANNIAICL CDIEOIMOMTS F I N A N C I A L C O M M O D I T I E S
PURECIOS SNTEOS P R E C I O U S S T O N E S
FSORET PDRUCTOS F O R E S T P R O D U C T S
TSOF CMOEDITMIOS S O F T C O M M O D I T I E S
LVETCOSIK DAN EATM L I V E S T O C K A N D M E A T
ELMTA M E T A L
ARIRUGULTCE A G R I C U L T U R E
EGRNEY E N E R G Y

## A.K. Scramble Puzzle #3d p. 55

Scramble Puzzle #3d - Trading Instruments - Solution

Uncramble the Types of Stocks in the list below

| | |
|---|---|
| DFEIENVSE SKCTOS | DEFENSIVE STOCKS |
| DNIEIVDD SKCTOS | DIVIDEND STOCKS |
| UEVAL SKTOCS | VALUE STOCKS |
| GOTRWH SKCTOS | GROWTH STOCKS |
| YNPEN SOCKTS | PENNY STOCKS |
| BUECLI-HP SKCTOS | BLUE-CHIP STOCKS |
| PERERFRED COSKT | PREFERRED STOCK |
| CMOMON SKTOCS | COMMON STOCKS |

## A.K. Definition Match-Up #3a p. 56

**SOLUTION**

1. D
2. H
3. G
4. E
5. A
6. B
7. C
8. F

## A.K. Definition Match-Up #3b p. 57

**SOLUTION**

1. E
2. H
3. G
4. F
5. B
6. A
7. D
8. C

## A.K. Definition Match-Up #3c p. 58

**SOLUTION**

1. F
2. H
3. B
4. G
5. A
6. C
7. E
8. D

## A.K. Definition Match-Up #3d p. 59

**SOLUTION**

1. D
2. H
3. A
4. G
5. B
6. F
7. C
8. E

## A.K. Cloze Test #3a p. 60

**SOLUTION**

1. a) Stocks
2. h) CFDs
3. b) Options
4. f) Commodities
5. d) ETFs
6. g) Bonds
7. e) Currencies
8. c) Futures

## A.K. Cloze Test #3b p. 61

**SOLUTION**

1. a) Stocks
2. d) Futures
3. c) Options
4. h) Convertible bonds
5. g) Warrants
6. e) Mutual funds
7. f) ETFs
8. b) Bonds

## A.K. Cloze Test #3c p. 62

**SOLUTION**

1. h) Financial commodities
2. g) Agriculture
3. a) Livestock and meat
4. f) Energy
5. e) Precious stones
6. d) Metal
7. c) Soft commodities
8. b) Forest products

## A.K. Cloze Test #3d p. 63

**SOLUTION**

1. d) Penny stocks
2. f) Defensive stocks
3. e) Growth stocks
4. c) Blue-chip stocks
5. g) Dividend stocks
6. b) Preferred stocks
7. a) Common stocks
8. f) Value stocks

| A.K. Missing Vowel #3a p. 64 | A.K. Missing Vowel #3b p. 65 |
| --- | --- |
| **Missing Vowel #3a**<br>Learn about Trading Instruments in the Stock Market<br>Currencies<br>Commodities<br>Bonds<br>Stocks<br>Options<br>Futures<br>Etfs<br>Contracts For Difference | **Missing Vowel #3b**<br>Learn about Types of Securities in the Stock Market<br>Mutual Funds<br>Convertible Bonds<br>Warrants<br>Etfs<br>Futures<br>Options<br>Bonds<br>Stocks |
| **A.K. Missing Vowel #3c p. 66** | **A.K. Missing Vowel #3d p. 67** |
| **Missing Vowel #3c**<br>Learn about Types of Commodities in the Stock Market<br>Financial Commodities<br>Precious Stones<br>Forest Products<br>Soft Commodities<br>Livestock And Meat<br>Metal<br>Energy | **Missing Vowel #3d**<br>Learn about Types of Stocks in the Stock Market<br>Penny Stocks<br>Growth Stocks<br>Value Stocks<br>Defensive Stocks<br>Dividend Stocks<br>Blue-Chip Stocks<br>Preferred Stock<br>Common Stocks |

## A.K. Double Puzzle #3a p. 68

### Double Puzzle #3a - Solution

A list of words that describe the Trading Instruments in the Stock Market

SCTKOS STOCKS

OTNPIOS OPTIONS

FERUUTS FUTURES

TFSE ETFS

CRICUEENRS CURRENCIES

CEMIMODOTIS COMMODITIES

DSBON BONDS

DCSF CFDS

THE FUNNIEST THING ABOUT TRADING INSTRUMENTS IS THAT THEY OFTEN HAVE HUMOROUS NAMES, SUCH AS PORK BELLY FUTURES AND BUTTERFLY SPREAD OPTIONS.

## A.K. Double Puzzle #3b p. 69

### Double Puzzle #3b - Solution

A list of words that describe the Types of Securities in the Stock Market

SBOND BONDS

CTONVBRELIE SBOND CONVERTIBLE BONDS

MAUUTL DFUSN MUTUAL FUNDS

WRARNTAS WARRANTS

SFET ETFS

OIONPTS OPTIONS

SKTOCS STOCKS

FRUTEUS FUTURES

SECURITIES ARE ESSENTIALLY JUST PIECES OF PAPER WITH NUMBERS WRITTEN ON THEM, YET PEOPLE ACT LIKE THEY'RE WORTH A FORTUNE.

## A.K. Double Puzzle #3c p. 70

### Double Puzzle #3c - Solution

A list of words that describe the Types of Commodities in the Stock Market

FAINAICNL CIITMEOODMS FINANCIAL COMMODITIES

ERGENY ENERGY

ELMTA METAL

AUURGLTRICE AGRICULTURE

LCTSIOEVK NDA AMTE LIVESTOCK AND MEAT

FTOS CEDTMIIOOMS SOFT COMMODITIES

PEOIRUCS SOETNS PRECIOUS STONES

FRESOT PCTORDUS FOREST PRODUCTS

THE VALUE OF TANGIBLE COMMODITIES IS DETERMINED BY INTANGIBLE FACTORS.

## A.K. Double Puzzle #3d p. 71

### Double Puzzle #3d - Solution

A list of words that describe the Types of Stocks in the Stock Market

PERRFEERD SCKOTS PREFERRED STOCKS

CMMOON SOCKTS COMMON STOCKS

BC-IEHULP SCTKOS BLUE-CHIP STOCKS

GOTRWH SOKTCS GROWTH STOCKS

EUAVL SOCKTS VALUE STOCKS

DVEDNIID SOCKTS DIVIDEND STOCKS

DFEISEVNE SKTOCS DEFENSIVE STOCKS

NYPEN SKTOCS PENNY STOCKS

INVESTING IN STOCKS IS BUYING A TINY SLICE OF A PIE HOPING IT BECOMES A WHOLE CAKE.

## A.K. Cryptograms #3 p. 72

1. TRADING INSTRUMENTS, SUCH AS STOCKS AND BONDS, CAN BE A VALUABLE WAY TO DIVERSIFY AN INVESTMENT PORTFOLIO AND POTENTIALLY EARN A FINANCIAL RETURN.

2. INVESTING IN SECURITIESCAN PROVIDE INDIVIDUALS AND BUSINESSES WITH THE OPPORTUNITY TO POTENTIALLY GROW THEIR WEALTH OVER TIME.

3. SOME INVESTORS USE COMMODITIES, SUCH AS GOLD AND SILVER, AS A HEDGE AGAINST INFLATION AND ECONOMIC UNCERTAINTY.

4. SOME STOCKS, SUCH AS THOSE OF BLUE-CHIP COMPANIES, ARE KNOWN FOR THEIR STABILITY AND STEADY RETURNS, WHILE OTHERS, SUCH AS THOSE OF HIGH-RISK STARTUPS, CAN BE MORE VOLATILE.

## A.K. Double Puzzle #3b p. 73

### Double Puzzle #3b - Solution

A list of words that describe the Types of Securities in the Stock Market

| | |
|---|---|
| SBOND | BONDS |
| CTONVBRELIE SBOND | CONVERTIBLE BONDS |
| MAUUTL DFUSN | MUTUAL FUNDS |
| WRARNTAS | WARRANTS |
| SFET | ETFS |
| OIONPTS | OPTIONS |
| SKTOCS | STOCKS |
| FRUTEUS | FUTURES |

SECURITIES ARE ESSENTIALLY JUST PIECES OF PAPER WITH NUMBERS WRITTEN ON THEM, YET PEOPLE ACT LIKE THEY'RE WORTH A FORTUNE.

## A.K. Double Puzzle #3c p. 74

### Double Puzzle #3c - Solution

A list of words that describe the Types of Commodities in the Stock Market

| | |
|---|---|
| FAINAICNL CIITMEOODMS | FINANCIAL COMMODITIES |
| ERGENY | ENERGY |
| ELMTA | METAL |
| AUURGLTRICE | AGRICULTURE |
| LCTSIOEVK NDA AMTE | LIVESTOCK AND MEAT |
| FTOS CEDTMIIOOMS | SOFT COMMODITIES |
| PEOIRUCS SOETNS | PRECIOUS STONES |
| FRESOT PCTORDUS | FOREST PRODUCTS |

THE VALUE OF TANGIBLE COMMODITIES IS DETERMINED BY INTANGIBLE FACTORS.

## A.K. Double Puzzle #3d p. 75

### Double Puzzle #3d - Solution

A list of words that describe the Types of Stocks in the Stock Market

| | |
|---|---|
| PERRFEERD SCKOTS | PREFERRED STOCKS |
| CMMOON SOCKTS | COMMON STOCKS |
| BC-IEHULP SCTKOS | BLUE-CHIP STOCKS |
| GOTRWH SOKTCS | GROWTH STOCKS |
| EUAVL SOCKTS | VALUE STOCKS |
| DVEDNIID SOCKTS | DIVIDEND STOCKS |
| DFEISEVNE SKTOCS | DEFENSIVE STOCKS |
| NYPEN SKTOCS | PENNY STOCKS |

INVESTING IN STOCKS IS BUYING A TINY SLICE OF A PIE HOPING IT BECOMES A WHOLE CAKE.

## A.K. Related Words #3a p. 76

**SOLUTION**

1. D) CFDs
2. A) Commodities
3. H) Currencies
4. B) Bonds
5. C) Futures
6. E) ETFs
7. G) Options
8. F) Stocks

## A.K. Related Words #3b p. 77

**SOLUTION**

1. F) Options
2. G) Futures
3. A) Mutual funds
4. B) ETFs
5. H) Warrants
6. C) Convertible bonds
7. E) Stocks
8. D) Bonds

## A.K. Related Words #3c p. 78

**SOLUTION**

1. D) Financial commodities
2. H) Agriculture
3. F) Energy
4. G) Metal
5. B) Livestock and meat
6. C) Soft commodities
7. E) Forest products
8. A) Precious stones

## A.K. Related Words #3d p. 79

**SOLUTION**

1. E) Common stocks
2. G) Preferred stocks
3. A) Blue-chip stocks
4. B) Penny stocks
5. H) Growth stocks
6. F) Value stocks
7. D) Dividend stocks
8. C) Defensive stocks

| A.K. Multiple-Choice Quiz #3a pp. 80-81 | A.K. Multiple-Choice Quiz #3b pp. 82-83 |
|---|---|
| **SOLUTION**<br><br>1. d<br>2. b<br>3. a<br>4. d<br>5. b<br>6. b<br>7. a<br>8. c<br>9. a<br>10. b | **SOLUTION**<br><br>1. a<br>2. b<br>3. a<br>4. a<br>5. c<br>6. b<br>7. a<br>8. b<br>9. a<br>10. b |
| **A.K. Multiple-Choice Quiz #3c pp. 84-85** | **A.K. Multiple-Choice Quiz #3d pp. 86-87** |
| **SOLUTION**<br><br>1. a<br>2. b<br>3. a<br>4. a<br>5. a<br>6. b<br>7. a<br>8. a<br>9. a<br>10. a | **SOLUTION**<br><br>1. a<br>2. b<br>3. c<br>4. d<br>5. b<br>6. c<br>7. d<br>8. d<br>9. b<br>10. d |

## A.K. Word Search Puzzle #4 p. 92

Word Search Puzzle #4 - Different Types of Trading - Solution

| M | | S | | | | | | | | | | | | P | T |
|---|---|---|---|---|---|---|---|---|---|---|---|---|---|---|---|
| O | O | | W | | | | | | | | | | | O | E |
| M | V | P | S | I | | | | | | | | | | S | C |
| E | D | A | T | C | N | | | | | | | | | I | H |
| N | | A | L | I | A | G | | | | | | | | T | N |
| T | | | Y | U | O | L | T | | | | | | | I | I |
| U | | | | T | E | N | P | R | | | | | | O | C |
| M | | | | | R | I | S | I | A | | | | | N | A |
| T | | | | | | A | N | T | N | D | | | | T | L |
| R | | | | | | | D | V | R | G | I | | | R | T |
| A | | | | | | | | I | E | A | | N | | A | R |
| D | | | | | | | | | N | S | D | | G | D | A |
| I | | | | | | | | | | G | T | I | | I | D |
| N | | | | | | | | | | | | I | N | N | I |
| G | | | | | | | | | | | | | N | G | N |
| | | | | | | | | | | | | | | G | G |

## A.K. Crossword Puzzle #4 p. 93

# Crossword Puzzle #4

Learn about Trading Types

[1→] Day Trading
[2↓] Swing Trading
[3→] Position Trading
[4↓] Scalping
[5→] Value Investing
[6↓] Options Trading
[7↓] Penny Stock Trading
[8→] Fundamental Trading
[9↓] Momentum Trading
[10→] Technical Trading

## A.K. Scramble #4 p. 94

Scramble Puzzle #4 - Different Trading Types - Solution

Uncramble the different trading types in the list below

AYD TNIRDAG — DAY TRADING
TICEACNHL TNIRDAG — TECHNICAL TRADING
FAMNDUNEATL TADNRIG — FUNDAMENTAL TRADING
PIISOOTN TDRINAG — POSITION TRADING
MNTOMUEM TDINRAG — MOMENTUM TRADING
GNSIW TDIANRG — SWING TRADING
OOPNITS TNIARDG — OPTIONS TRADING
ULVEA INTSINVEG — VALUE INVESTING
NYEPN COSKT TNRADIG — PENNY STOCK TRADING
SICANPLG — SCALPING

## A.K. Definition Match-up Quiz #4 p. 95

**SOLUTION**

1- G) Momentum trading
2- E) Swing trading
3- F) Day trading
4- B) Position trading
5- A) Scalping
6- H) Options trading
7- J) Technical trading
8- D) Fundamental trading
9- C) Value investing
10- I) Penny stock trading

## A.K. Cloze Test #4 p. 96

### Cloze Test #4 - SOLUTION

**Fill In the Banks Using the 10 Trading Types below:**

a) Day trading - b) Swing trading - c) Position trading - d) Scalping - e) Momentum trading - f) Value investing - g) Options trading - h) Penny stock trading - i) Fundamental trading j) Technical trading

There are many different approaches to trading in the stock market, and each approach has its own set of advantages and disadvantages. a)**Day trading** is when you buy and sell stocks within the same trading day, while b) **swing trading** is when you hold onto a stock for a few days to a few weeks. c) **Position trading** is when you hold onto a stock for a longer period of time, usually months to a year. d) **Scalping** is a type of day trading where you try to make a small profit by buying and selling a stock multiple times within the same day. e) **Momentum trading** is when you buy stocks that are gaining momentum, or increasing in price quickly. f) **Value investing** is when you buy stocks that are undervalued by the market, with the hope that their value will increase in the future. g) **Options trading**, h) **penny stock trading**, i) **fundamental trading**, and j) **technical trading** are also different ways of approaching the stock market, each with its own set of risks and rewards. Ultimately, the key is to understand your goals, risk tolerance, and the different strategies available to you, so you can make informed decisions and find the approach that works best for you.

N.B. The order of the answers from g) to j) is interchangeable. 147

## A.K. Missing Vowel #4 p. 97

# Missing Vowel #4

Learn about Different Trading Types

Value Investing
Technical Trading
Swing Trading
Scalping
Position Trading
Penny Stock Trading
Options Trading
Momentum Trading
Fundamental Trading
Day Trading

## A.K. Multiple-Choice #4 pp. 98-99

**SOLUTION**

1. A
2. B
3. A
4. A
5. C
6. B
7. A
8. B
9. A
10. B

## A.K. Double Puzzle #4 p. 100

### Double Puzzle #4 - Solution

A list of words that describe different Trading Types in the Stock Market

| | |
|---|---|
| AYD TADINRG | DAY TRADING |
| WINGS TDRINAG | SWING TRADING |
| PSITOOIN TINRADG | POSITION TRADING |
| SALICNPG | SCALPING |
| MMNTUOEM TANIRDG | MOMENTUM TRADING |
| LVUEA ITENVISNG | VALUE INVESTING |
| OINTPOS TADINRG | OPTIONS TRADING |
| YNPEN TKSOC TDINRAG | PENNY STOCK TRADING |
| FENAMUTDANL TNRIADG | FUNDAMENTAL TRADING |
| THICENACL TINRADG | TECHNICAL TRADING |

APPROXIMATELY 70% OF TRADING VOLUME ON US STOCK MARKETS IS GENERATED BY ALGORITHMIC OR HIGH-FREQUENCY TRADERS, ALSO KNOWN AS ROBOTS.

## A.K. Cryptogram #4 p. 101

**1.** THERE ARE COUNTRIES IN THE WORLD THAT HAVE NO STOCK MARKET AT ALL SUCH AS NORTH KOREA, CUBA, AND SYRIA.

## A.K. Related Words #4 p. 102

**SOLUTION**

1. B) Position trading
2. E) Value investing
3. H) Fundamental trading
4. F) Options trading
5. I) Technical trading
6. D) Momentum trading
7. C) Scalping
8. J) Swing trading
9. G) Penny stock trading
10. A) Day trading

## A.K. Word Search Puzzle #5a p. 107

Word Search Puzzle #5a - Bull and Bear Markets - Solution

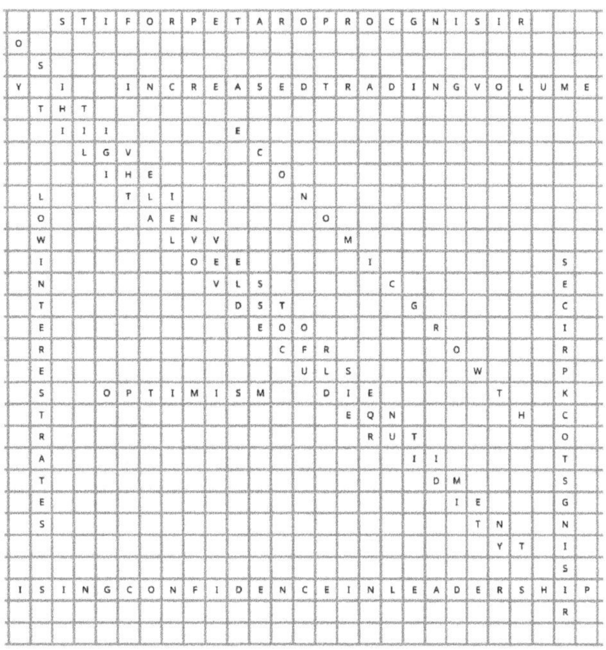

## A.K. Word Search Puzzle #5b p. 108

Word Search Puzzle #5b - Bull and Bear Markets - Solution

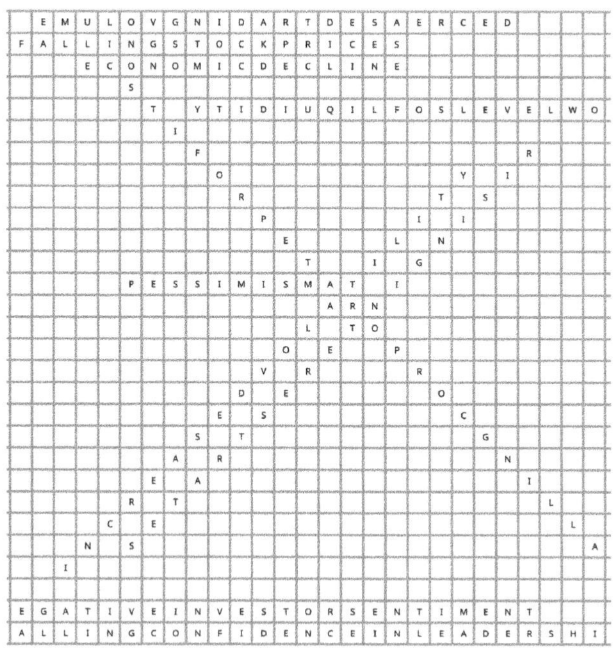

## A.K. Crossword Puzzle #5a p. 109

### Crossword Puzzle #5a - Bull and Bear Markets

Learn about the characteristics of Bull Markets in the list below:

[1↓] Optimism
[2→] Confidence
[3↓] Liquidity
[4→] Stability
[5→] Low Rates
[6↓] Profits
[7↓] Growth
[8↓] Bullish
[9→] High Volume
[10→] Bull Market

## A.K. Crossword Puzzle #5b p. 110

### Crossword Puzzle #5b - Bull and Bear Markets

Learn about the characteristics of Bear Markets in the list below:

[1→] Pessimism
[2↓] Distrust
[3→] Low Liquidity
[4↓] Volatility
[5→] High Rates
[6→] Lower Profits
[7↓] Decline
[8↓] Bearish
[9↓] Low Volume
[10→] Bear Market

## A.K. Scramble Puzzle #5a p. 111

### Scramble Puzzle #5a - Trading Instruments - Solution

**Uncramble the Bull Market characteristics in the list below**

| | |
|---|---|
| EMIOONCC GTWROH | ECONOMIC GROWTH |
| OMPTSIIM | OPTIMISM |
| OWL IENTSRET ERSTA | LOW INTEREST RATES |
| RSNIIG COAORRTPE PITOFRS | RISING CORPORATE PROFITS |
| BLLISUH SIEEMNNTT | BULLISH SENTIMENT |
| HHIG LLEVES FO LUIDQTIIY | HIGH LEVELS OF LIQUIDITY |
| CCEOFNINDE NI LHISADEERP | CONFIDENCE IN LEADERSHIP |
| IESARNECD TINRADG VUOMLE | INCREASED TRADING VOLUME |
| RINSIG TKSOC PCEIRS | RISING STOCK PRICES |
| RCEDEUD VLIIOTTALY | REDUCED VOLATILITY |

## A.K. Scramble Puzzle #5b p. 112

### Scramble Puzzle #5b - Trading Instruments - Solution

**Uncramble the Bear Market characteristics in the list below**

| | |
|---|---|
| EOMCINOC DLNCEIE | ECONOMIC DECLINE |
| PMIISSESM | PESSIMISM |
| FLNLAIG CKSTO PCEIRS | FALLING STOCK PRICES |
| RINSIG ITEESRNT SERTA | RISING INTEREST RATES |
| FLIANLG CAORTOPRE POITFRS | FALLING CORPORATE PROFITS |
| BISAREH SITEMNNET | BEARISH SENTIMENT |
| OWL LLEEVS FO LQDIITIUY | LOW LEVELS OF LIQUIDITY |
| IERESCAND VTAOIITLLY | INCREASED VOLATILITY |
| DEAEERCSD TNRADIG VUOMLE | DECREASED TRADING VOLUME |
| DRSISTUT NI LIERESADHP | DISTRUST IN LEADERSHIP |

| A.K. Definition Match-Up #5a p. 113 | A.K. Definition Match-Up #5b p. 114 |
|---|---|
| **SOLUTION**<br><br>1- D) Economic growth<br>2- E) Rising corporate profits<br>3- C) Bullish sentiment<br>4- J) Optimism about future growth<br>5- F) Low interest rates<br>6- A) Raising stock prices<br>7- B) Increased trading volume<br>8- H) High levels of liquidity<br>9- I) Rising confidence in leadership<br>10- G) Reduced volatility | **SOLUTION**<br><br>1- G) Increased volatility<br>2- D) Economic decline<br>3- E) Falling corporate profits:<br>4- F) Rising interest rates:<br>5- C) Bearish sentiment:<br>6- B) Decreased trading volume:<br>7- A) Falling stock prices<br>8- J) Pessimism about future growth<br>9- I) Falling confidence in leadership<br>10- H) Low levels of liquidity |
| **A.K. Cloze Test #5a p. 115** | **A.K. Cloze Test #5b p. 116** |
| **Bull Market Characteristics**<br><br>a) economic growth<br>b) rising corporate profits<br>c) bullish sentiment<br>d) optimism<br>e) Low interest rates<br>f) Rising stock prices<br>g) increased trading volume<br>h) high levels of liquidity<br>i) rising confidence in leadership<br>j) reduced volatility | **Bear Market Characteristics**<br><br>a) economic decline<br>b) falling stock prices<br>c) falling corporate profits<br>d) Bearish sentiment<br>e) pessimism about future growth<br>f) Rising interest rates<br>g) decreased trading volume<br>h) low levels of liquidity<br>i) Falling confidence in leadership<br>j) increased volatility |

## A.K. Missing Vowel #5a p. 117

# Missing Vowel #5a

Learn about Bull Market Characteristics

Stock Prices Going Up
More Trading
Positive Attitude
Economic Growth
Companies Making More Money
Low Borrowing Costs
Fewer Ups And Downs
Plenty Of Money To Invest
Leadership Is Trusted
Hope For The Future

## A.K. Missing Vowel #5b p. 118

# Missing Vowel #5b

Learn about Bear Market Characteristics

Stock Prices Going Down
Less Trading
Negative Attitude
Economic Decline
Companies Making Less Money
High Borrowing Costs
More Ups And Downs
Less Money To Invest
Leadership Is Not Trusted
No Hope For The Future

## A.K. Double Puzzle #5a p. 119

### Double Puzzle #5a - Solution

A list of words that describe characterictics of Bull Markets

EOOIMNCC GTWROH — ECONOMIC GROWTH
OSIMIPTM — OPTIMISM
OWL ITESENRT ASERT — LOW INTEREST RATES
RIINSG POTRFIS — RISING PROFITS
BLSULIH SNIETNEMT — BULLISH SENTIMENT
IHHG LDITIQUIY — HIGH LIQUIDITY
RNIISG CDOINECFNE — RISING CONFIDENCE
TNIRDAG VUMLOE PU — TRADING VOLUME UP
RSINIG TCKOS PICERS — RISING STOCK PRICES
RUCEEDD VITLATOILY — REDUCED VOLATILITY

BULL MARKETS TEND TO LAST LONGER AND TO BE MORE PROFITABLE THAN BEAR MARKETS, WITH BULL MARKETS TYPICALLY GAINING MORE THAN DOUBLE THE AMOUNT OF THE LOSSES IN BEAR MARKETS.

## A.K. Double Puzzle #5b p. 120

### Double Puzzle #5b - Solution

A list of words that describe characterictics of Bear Markets

PSESISMIM — PESSIMISM
FNAILLG KCTSO PERICS — FALLING STOCK PRICES
RNIISG IENETSRT AESTR — RISING INTEREST RATES
FIALNLG PTRIOFS — FALLING PROFITS
BSRIEAH SNIEMTENT — BEARISH SENTIMENT
WLO LTIIQIDUY — LOW LIQUIDITY
ICRSNEAED VIITOLTALY — INCREASED VOLATILITY
TDRINAG VUMLOE NDOW — TRADING VOLUME DOWN

BEAR MARKETS TEND TO BE MORE VOLATILE THAN BULL MARKETS, WITH MARKETS TYPICALLY DROPPING MORE THAN DOUBLE THE AMOUNT OF THE GAINS IN BULL MARKETS.

| A.K. Cryptogram #5a p. 121 | A.K. Cryptogram #5b p. 122 |
|---|---|
| 1. BULL MARKETS OFTEN LEAD TO EUPHORIA, SPECULATION AND MARKET BUBBLES WHICH CAN BE BOTH DANGEROUS AND DAMAGING WHEN THEY EVENTUALLY BURST. | 2. BEAR MARKETS, THOUGH DIFFICULT IN THE SHORT-TERM, HAVE BEEN FOLLOWED BY HIGHER RETURNS IN THE STOCK MARKET OVER THE LONG-TERM, AS THE MARKET HAS ALWAYS HISTORICALLY RECOVERED AND REACHED NEW HIGHS. |
| **Related Words Match-Up #5a p. 123** | **Related Words Match-Up #5b p. 124** |
| **SOLUTION**<br><br>1. E) Optimism<br>2. C) Low interest rates<br>3. A) Rising corporate profits<br>4. D) Positive investor sentiment<br>5. G) High levels of liquidity<br>6. F) Rising confidence in leadership<br>7. H) Increased trading volume<br>8. I) Rising stock prices<br>9. J) Reduced volatility<br>10. B) Economic growth | **SOLUTION**<br><br>1. D) Pessimism<br>2. F) Falling stock prices<br>3. C) Rising interest rates<br>4. B) Falling corporate profits<br>5. G) Negative investor sentiment<br>6. A) Low levels of liquidity<br>7. H) Increased volatility<br>8. I) Decreased trading volume<br>9. J) Falling confidence in leadership<br>10. E) Economic decline |

| A.K. Multiple-Choice Quiz #5a p. 126 | A.K. Multiple-Choice Quiz #5b p. 128 |
|---|---|

**SOLUTION** (Quiz #5a)

1. b
2. c
3. b
4. c
5. b
6. d
7. b
8. a
9. d
10. a

**SOLUTION** (Quiz #5b)

1. b
2. c
3. b
4. a
5. d
6. a
7. c
8. a
9. d
10. a

## Word Search Puzzle #6 p. 132

Word Search Puzzle #6 - Solution

| S | G | N | I | N | R | A | E | D | N | A | E | U | N | E | V | E | R |  | A |
|---|---|---|---|---|---|---|---|---|---|---|---|---|---|---|---|---|---|---|---|
|  |  |  |  |  |  |  |  |  |  |  |  |  |  |  |  | S |  |  | S |
|  |  | O |  |  |  |  |  |  |  |  |  |  |  |  |  | N |  |  | S |
| E | Y | T | I | U | Q | E | N | O | N | R | U | T | E | R |  | I |  |  | E |
| R |  |  |  | T |  |  |  |  |  |  |  |  |  |  |  | G |  |  | T |
| A |  |  |  |  | A |  |  |  |  |  |  |  |  |  |  | R |  |  | A |
| H |  |  |  |  |  | R |  |  |  |  |  |  |  |  |  | A |  |  | N |
| S |  |  |  |  |  |  | Y |  |  |  |  |  |  |  | F | M |  |  | D |
| R |  |  |  |  |  |  |  | T |  |  |  |  | R |  |  | T |  |  | L |
| E |  |  |  |  |  |  |  |  | I |  |  | E |  |  |  | I |  |  | I |
| P |  |  |  |  |  |  |  |  |  | U | E |  |  |  |  | F |  |  | A |
| S |  |  |  |  |  |  |  |  |  | C | Q |  |  |  |  | O |  |  | B |
| G |  |  |  |  |  |  |  |  | A |  |  | E |  |  |  | R |  |  | I |
| N |  |  |  |  |  |  |  | S |  |  |  |  | O |  |  | P |  |  | L |
| I |  |  |  |  |  |  | H |  |  |  |  |  |  | T |  |  |  |  | I |
| N |  |  |  |  |  | F |  |  |  |  |  |  |  |  | T |  |  |  | T |
| R |  |  |  |  | L |  |  |  |  |  |  |  |  |  |  | B |  |  | Y |
| A |  |  |  | O |  |  |  |  |  |  |  |  |  |  |  |  | E |  |  |
| E |  |  | W |  |  |  |  |  |  |  |  |  |  |  |  |  |  | D |  |
|  |  | D | I | V | I | D | E | N | D | Y | I | E | L | D |  |  |  |  |  |

## Crossword Puzzle #6 p. 133

# Crossword Puzzle #6

Learn about Fundamental Analysis

[1→] Revenue And Earnings
[2↓] Profit Margins
[3→] Asset And Liability
[4→] Debt-To-Equity Ratio
[5→] Return On Equity
[6↓] Price-To-Earnings Ratio
[7↓] Dividend Yield
[8↓] Earnings Per Share
[9↓] Free Cash Flow
[10→] Market Capitalization

## A.K. Scramble Puzzle #6 p. 134

### Scramble Puzzle #6 - Fundamental Analysis - Solution

Uncramble the different key concepts in the list below

| | |
|---|---|
| POFIRT MGNRAIS | PROFIT MARGINS |
| RRETUN NO EITUQY | RETURN ON EQUITY |
| TESAS DAN LLIIBATIY | ASSET AND LIABILITY |
| EIGNRANS RPE HAESR | EARNINGS PER SHARE |
| PIN-AEEGONCIR-RTS AORTI | PRICE-TO-EARNINGS RATIO |
| EERF AHCS OWLF | FREE CASH FLOW |
| DO-IBTUTQTEE-Y ORATI | DEBT-TO-EQUITY RATIO |
| REUNVEE NDA ENNIGRAS | REVENUE AND EARNINGS |
| MKAERT CZLIAPIOTTIAAN | MARKET CAPITALIZATION |
| DNEVIIDD IEDYL | DIVIDEND YIELD |

## A.K. Definition Match-Up #6 p. 135

**SOLUTION**

1- H) Earnings Per Share (EPS)
2- F) Price-to-Earnings Ratio (P/E ratio)
3- C) Asset and Liability
4- A) Revenue and Earnings
5- B) Profit Margins
6- I) Free Cash Flow
7- J) Market Capitalization
8- E) Return on Equity (ROE)
9- D) Debt-to-Equity Ratio
10- G) Dividend Yield

## Cloze Test #6 p. 136

**Fundamental Analysis**

a) Revenue and Earnings
b) Profit Margins
c) Asset and Liability
d) Debt-to-Equity Ratio
e) Return on Equity (ROE)
f) Price-to-Earnings Ratio (P/E ratio)
g) Dividend Yield
h) Earnings Per Share (EPS)
i) Free Cash Flow
j) Market Capitalization

## Missing Vowel #6 p. 137

### Missing Vowel #6 - Solution

Learn about Fundamental Analysis

| | |
|---|---|
| PROFIT MARGINS | A measure of a company's profitability, calculated by dividing net income by revenue. |
| ASSET AND LIABILITY | A company's resources and debt levels are shown by its assets and liabilities. |
| DEBT-TO-EQUITY RATIO | A measure of a company's leverage, compares total liabilities to total equity. |
| RETURN ON EQUITY | (ROE) A measure of a company's profitability from shareholders' investments. |
| PRICE-TO-EARNINGS RATIO | (P/E ratio) A measure of a company's valuation, compares stock price to earnings per share. |
| DIVIDEND YIELD | A measure of dividends paid to shareholders relative to stock price. |
| EARNINGS PER SHARE | (EPS) A measure of a company's profitability, calculated by dividing net income by outstanding shares. |
| FREE CASH FLOW | Cash generated after accounting for capital expenditures, important for paying dividends or investing in growth. |
| MARKET CAPITALIZATION | The total value of a company's outstanding shares, used to classify companies by size. |
| REVENUE AND EARNINGS | A company's financial performance and future growth potential are shown by its revenue and earnings. |

## A.K. Double Puzzle #6 p. 138

### Double Puzzle #6 - Solution

A list of words that describe concepts of Fundamental Analysis

| | |
|---|---|
| ERNIGANS ERP HERSA | EARNINGS PER SHARE |
| PNEONI A-CGERRTIS IRAOT | PRICE-TO-EARNINGS RATIO |
| ESATS DAN LBTAIIILY | ASSET AND LIABILITY |
| RVUEENE NDA EGIRANNS | REVENUE AND EARNINGS |
| POFIRT MGINARS | PROFIT MARGINS |
| REFE HCAS WOFL | FREE CASH FLOW |
| MKERAT CLAZIIAPAITOTN | MARKET CAPITALIZATION |
| RTUREN NO EITUQY | RETURN ON EQUITY |
| DETIOBTQ-ET-UY IRAOT | DEBT-TO-EQUITY RATIO |
| DDNEVIID LEYDI | DIVIDEND YIELD |

WARREN BUFFETT, WHO IS WIDELY CONSIDERED ONE OF THE GREATEST INVESTORS OF ALL TIME, IS A BIG PROPONENT OF FUNDAMENTAL ANALYSIS. HE HAS SAID THAT HE READS 500 PAGES OF ANNUAL REPORTS EVERY DAY AND THAT "FUNDAMENTALS ARE THE BACKBONE OF INVESTING."

## A.K. Cryptogram #6 p. 139

1. FUNDAMENTAL ANALYSIS OFTEN REQUIRES PATIENCE AND A LONG-TERM OUTLOOK, AS IT IS NOT ALWAYS POSSIBLE TO PREDICT THE SHORT-TERM PRICE MOVEMENTS OF A STOCK.

## Related Words Match-Up #6 p. 140

**SOLUTION**

1. H) Revenue and Earnings
2. F) Profit Margins
3. B) Asset and Liability
4. I) Debt-to-Equity Ratio
5. C) Return on Equity (ROE)
6. E) Price-to-Earnings Ratio (P/E ratio)
7. D) Dividend Yield
8. J) Earnings Per Share (EPS)
9. G) Free Cash Flow
10. A) Market Capitalization

## Multiple-Choice Quiz #6 p. 142

**SOLUTION**

1. d
2. c
3. a
4. d
5. a
6. b
7. a
8. d
9. c
10. c

## Word Search Puzzle #7 p. 146

Word Search Puzzle #7 - Technical Analysis - Solution

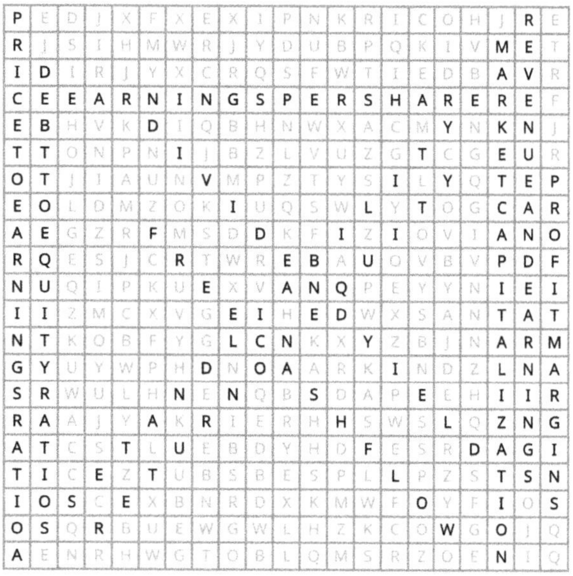

## Crossword Puzzle #7 p. 147

# Crossword Puzzle #7

Learn about Technical Analysis

[1↓] Chart Patterns
[2→] Indicators
[3→] Moving Averages
[4→] Support And Resistance
[5↓] Trend Lines
[6↓] Volatility
[7↓] Volume
[8↓] Overbought And Oversold
[9→] Divergence
[10→] Risk Management

## A.K. Scramble Puzzle #7 p. 148

Scramble Puzzle #7 - Technical Analysis - Solution

Uncramble the different key concepts in the list below

| | |
|---|---|
| EDNRT NLSIE | TREND LINES |
| OBRVUHGOET | OVERBOUGHT |
| OERSOLVD | OVERSOLD |
| VUOMLE | VOLUME |
| IIARONCDTS | INDICATORS |
| DEERVNGCIE | DIVERGENCE |
| MNIOVG AEVAGERS | MOVING AVERAGES |
| SORPPUT | SUPPORT |
| RCNSSAETIE | RESISTANCE |
| VLAITLITOY | VOLATILITY |
| RCHTA PEARNTTS | CHART PATTERNS |

## A.K. Definition Match-Up #7 p. 149

**SOLUTION**

1- a) Indicators
2- b) Moving averages
3- c) Chart patterns
4- d) Overbought and oversold
5- e) Risk management
6- f) Divergence
7- g) Support and resistance
8- i) Trend lines
9- j) Volatility
10- k) Volume

## A.K. Cloze Test #7 p. 150

**Technical Analysis**

a) Indicators
b) Moving Averages
c) Chart Patterns
d1) Overbought
d2) Oversold
e) Risk Management
f) Divergence
g1) Support
g2) Resistance
h) Volatility
i) Volume

## Missing Vowel Puzzle #7 p. 151

Missing Vowel #7 - Solution

Learn about Technical Analysis

| Answer | Clue |
|---|---|
| INDICATORS | Tools that give directions on when to buy or sell a stock. |
| MOVING AVERAGES | A filter that helps see the stock's trend more clearly. |
| CHART PATTERNS | Reading stock prices by its charts, to identify patterns that indicate a change in trend. |
| OVERBOUGHT AND OVERSOLD | When a stock's price has risen or fallen too fast. |
| RISK MANAGEMENT | Techniques to control and minimize potential losses and maximize potential gains of a trade. |
| DIVERGENCE | A difference between stock's price and an indicator that signals a change in trend. |
| SUPPORT AND RESISTANCE | Limits on how high or low a stock's price can go. |
| TREND LINES | Connecting price points to show the stock's current trend. |
| VOLATILITY | Measure of ups and downs in a stock's price. |
| VOLUME | Indicator of market sentiment towards a stock. |

## Double Puzzle #7 p. 152

Double Puzzle #7 - Solution

A list of words that describe concepts of Technical Analysis

| | |
|---|---|
| KRIS MNAEEMAGNT | RISK MANAGEMENT |
| IRIAONDTCS | INDICATORS |
| MNOVIG AEEAVRGS | MOVING AVERAGES |
| SPOPRUT NDA RSANCIESTE | SUPPORT AND RESISTANCE |
| RNDET SNELI | TREND LINES |
| HRCTA PETARNTS | CHART PATTERNS |
| DGECVNREIE | DIVERGENCE |
| VATILTOILY | VOLATILITY |
| VMUOLE | VOLUME |
| OEGBOVRHUT NDA OSOELVRD | OVERBOUGHT AND OVERSOLD |

"I NEVER USE VALUATION TO TIME THE MARKET. I USE LIQUIDITY CONSIDERATIONS AND TECHNICAL ANALYSIS FOR TIMING." - STANLEY DRUCKENMILLER

## A.K. Cryptogram Puzzle #7 p. 153

1. THIS BUSINESS IS NOT ABOUT INVESTING IN GREAT COMPANIES; IT'S ABOUT PROFITING FROM INEFFICIENTLY PRICED STOCKS. - Michael Lauer

| Related Words Match-Up #7 p. 154 | Multiple-Choice Quiz #7 p. 156 |
|---|---|

## Related Words Match-Up #7 p. 154

**SOLUTION**

1. Support and resistance J)
2. Divergence C)
3. Moving averages D)
4. Risk management I)
5. Volume A)
6. Trend lines E)
7. Overbought and oversold H)
8. Chart patterns F)
9. Indicators G)
10. Volatility B)

## Multiple-Choice Quiz #7 p. 156

**SOLUTION**

1. B
2. D
3. B
4. D
5. C
6. C
7. B
8. A
9. C
10. B

## Word Search Puzzle #8 p. 160

Word Search Puzzle #8 - Stock Market Idioms - Solution

| S | T | E | B | R | U | O | Y | E | G | D | E | H | | | |
|---|---|---|---|---|---|---|---|---|---|---|---|---|---|---|---|
| | S | | | | R | I | D | E | T | H | E | B | U | L | L |
| | E | | | | | | | | | | | | | | |
| | S | | | D | L | O | G | S | L | O | O | F | | | |
| | S | | T | | B | | | | | | | | | | |
| | O | | O | | L | | | | | | | | | | |
| | L | | T | | A | | | | | | | | | | |
| | S | | H | | C | | | | | | B | | | | |
| | E | | E | | K | | | | | | E | | | | |
| | N | | M | | S | | | | | | A | | | | |
| | O | | O | | W | | | | | | R | | | | |
| | T | | O | | A | | | | | | H | | | | |
| | U | | N | | N | | F | O | M | O | U | | | | |
| | C | | | | | | | | | | G | | | | |
| P | L | A | Y | T | H | E | M | A | R | K | E | T | | | |
| | | | | | | | | | | | | | | | |

## Crossword Puzzle #8 p. 161

# Crossword Puzzle #8

Learn about Stock Market Idioms

[1→] To The Moon
[2↓] Bear Hug
[3→] Ride The Bull
[4↓] Fomo
[5→] Hedge Your Bets
[6→] Sitting On Your Cash
[7↓] Cut One's Losses
[8→] Play The Market
[9↓] Black Swan
[10→] Fool's Gold

## A.K. Scramble Puzzle #8 p. 162

### Scramble Puzzle #8 - Stock Market Idioms - Solution

Uncramble the different stock market idioms in the list below

| | |
|---|---|
| FO'OLS LGDO | FOOL'S GOLD |
| TCU 'EOSN LSESOS | CUT ONE'S LOSSES |
| OT ETH OMNO | TO THE MOON |
| AREB UGH | BEAR HUG |
| EEGHD UYRO ETSB | HEDGE YOUR BETS |
| YPLA ETH MKERAT | PLAY THE MARKET |
| RAFE FO MSNIISG TOU | FEAR OF MISSING OUT |
| STTINIG NO OURY SCHA | SITTING ON YOUR CASH |
| IERD HET LLUB | RIDE THE BULL |
| LKCBA ANWS | BLACK SWAN |

## A.K. Definition Match-Up #8 p. 163

**SOLUTION**

1- E
2- I
3- J
4- H
5- A
6- G
7- B
8- C
9- F
10- B

## A.K. Cloze Test #8 p. 164

### Stock Market Idioms

a) hedging bets
b) fool's gold
c) ride the bull
d) FOMO
e) cutting losses
f) playing the market
g) bear hug
h) black swan
i) to the moon
j) sitting on her cash

## A.K. Missing Vowel #8 p. 165

### Missing Vowel #8 - Solution

Learn about Stock Market Idioms

| | |
|---|---|
| RIDE THE BULL | Taking advantage of rising market trends, expecting prices to go up. |
| HEDGE YOUR BETS | Diversifying investments to reduce risk by spreading assets. |
| CUT ONE'S LOSSES | Selling investments early to minimize losses. |
| FOOL'S GOLD | Investments that seem valuable but turn out to be worth much less. |
| SITTING ON YOUR CASH | Holding onto cash, waiting for the right opportunity to invest. |
| FOMO | Anxiety about missing profitable opportunities. |
| BLACK SWAN | Unexpected and rare events with a significant impact on markets. |
| PLAY THE MARKET | Engaging in buying, selling, or trading for profit. |
| TO THE MOON | Expecting a significant increase in a stock's price. |
| BEAR HUG | An aggressive strategy of persistently pursuing another company for acquisition. |

## Double Puzzle #8 p. 166

### Double Puzzle #8 - Solution

A list of idioms related to the stock market

| Scrambled | Solution | Numbered letters |
|---|---|---|
| EDRI ETH LBUL | RIDE THE BULL | 7 53 10 58 51 |
| GDHEE OURY ETSB | HEDGE YOUR BETS | 9 49 12 |
| TCU 'ESNO LSOESS | CUT ONE'S LOSSES | 29 59 23 52 42 |
| FO'OLS OLDG | FOOL'S GOLD | 20 30 11 8 60 |
| SNITTIG NO UYRO HCAS | SITTING ON YOUR CASH | 16 26 31 15 37 38 57 54 40 14 34 56 |
| MFOO | FOMO | 19 48 |
| KACBL ASNW | BLACK SWAN | 6 50 17 27 22 41 |
| YAPL HET MEKART | PLAY THE MARKET | 24 4 35 2 |
| OT HET NOMO | TO THE MOON | 33 3 61 |
| ABRE GHU | BEAR HUG | |

"THE BIGGEST RISK OF ALL IS NOT TAKING ONE." — MELLODY HOBSON

## A.K. Cryptogram #8 p. 167

1. PUMP AND DUMP IS A FRAUDULENT SCHEME IN THE STOCK MARKET WHERE THE PRICE OF A STOCK IS ARTIFICIALLY INFLATED, AND THEN THE SCHEMERS SELL OFF THEIR SHARES, LEAVING OTHER INVESTORS WITH LOSSES. - Anonymous

## A.K. Related Words Match-Up #88 p. 168

**SOLUTION**

1. FOMO H)
2. Play the market C)
3. To the moon G)
4. Hedge your bets I)
5. Bear hug A)
6. Fool's gold D)
7. Cut one's losses E)
8. Black swan B)
9. Sitting on your cash J)
10. Ride the bull F)

## Multiple-Choice Quiz #8 p. 170

**SOLUTION**

1. B
2. A
3. A
4. D
5. A
6. B
7. C
8. D
9. C
10. A

www.ingramcontent.com/pod-product-compliance
Lightning Source LLC
LaVergne TN
LVHW060036210926
848481LV00013B/3875

* 9 7 8 1 0 6 9 4 9 5 3 1 0 *